LOSING *Faith*

LEAVING *Ministry*

LOVING *God*

LOSING Faith
LEAVING Ministry
LOVING God

A Personal Pilgrimage
to the Isle of Iona

RALPH W. E. PATRICK

Losing Faith, Leaving Ministry, Loving God: A Personal Pilgrimage to the Isle of Iona
Published by The Celtic Compass
Denver, Colorado, U.S.A.

PATRICK, RALPH W.E., Author
LOSING FAITH, LEAVING MINISTRY, LOVING GOD
RALPH W.E. PATRICK

Library of Congress Control Number: 2024908343

ISBN: 979-8-9905490-0-5, 979-8-9905490-2-9 (paperback)
ISBN: 979-8-9905490-3-6 (hardcover)
ISBN: 979-8-9905490-1-2 (digital)

RELIGION / Christian Living / Calling & Vocation
RELIGION / Faith Deconstruction
BODY, MIND & SPIRIT / Inspiration & Personal Growth
RELIGION / Christian Ministry / Pastoral Resources
FAMILY & RELATIONSHIPS / Life Stages / Mid-Life

Editing: Bethany Good (goodwritingco.com)
Book Design: Michelle White (mmwbooks.com)
Publishing Consultant: Susie Schaefer (finishthebookpublishing.com)

QUANTITY PURCHASES:
Schools, companies, professional groups, clubs, and other organizations
may qualify for special terms when ordering quantities of this title.
For information, email hello@celticcompass.com.

For my parents, Ralph and Jean,
who gave me the greatest life any boy could ever dream of.
And for my daughters Katie, Kayleen, Meghan, and Molley,
who are the greatest gift a father could ever be given.

Table of Contents

The Power of Iona

In the year 563 AD, or thereabouts, Colm Cille, better known as Saint Columba, set foot on the rocky windswept shore of the island of Iona. Columba came to Iona a troubled soul, seeking to find meaning and purpose through a perilous mission to the wild people of what is modern-day Scotland. An unsettled life of strife and contention led him, and a small group of companions, to undertake a dangerous journey to this rocky island on the rugged and often stormy west coast of Scotland. On Iona, Columba found his meaning and purpose. His success in the mission to evangelize the people of Scotland is testimony to the invigorative power of Iona.

Since then, countless people of varied backgrounds and origins have come to this holy island on a virtual pilgrimage, seeking what Columba sought, and there found meaning and purpose in life. Ralph Patrick was one of those "pilgrims." Little did he know, when he first stepped off the ferry onto the stony shore, that Iona would become such an important factor in his life.

There is a mystic character in the rugged west coast of Scotland, enhanced by the fog, rain, and mist that frequently characterize the region. Speaking from my own experience, making the trek from Oban to Mull and the final ferry to Iona, one finds that the first step off the dock into a place of spiritual power is something one never forgets.

Ralph Patrick's struggles as a Lutheran pastor, his having to deal with difficult assignments, with care and concern for his family, and finally, the death of his mother and marital problems brought him to return to Iona more than once, seeking renewal and spiritual revitalization. His spiritual struggles raised doubts at many levels including serious questions about faith and ministry. His intriguing story is one of spiritual struggle to find peace and fulfillment, like the Old Testament account of Jacob wrestling with the Angel of God (Genesis 32:24–28). Patrick's wrestling with God led him on many paths, but ultimately led to his final return to Iona, where he found new meaning and purpose—and, I believe, a new understanding of God and priesthood.

The V. Rev. Lester Michael Bundy,
Professor Emeritus, Regis University

Introduction

A JOURNEY INTO THE SECOND HALF OF OUR OWN LIVES
AWAITS US ALL. NOT EVERYBODY GOES THERE, EVEN THOUGH
ALL OF US GET OLDER, AND SOME OF US GET OLDER THAN OTHERS.
A 'FURTHER JOURNEY' IS A WELL-KEPT SECRET, FOR SOME REASON.
MANY PEOPLE DO NOT EVEN KNOW THERE IS ONE. THERE ARE
TOO FEW WHO ARE AWARE OF IT, TELL US ABOUT IT, OR KNOW THAT
IT IS DIFFERENT FROM THE JOURNEY OF THE FIRST HALF OF LIFE.
—Richard Rohr, *Falling Upward*

I know about the journey Richard Rohr speaks of in *Falling Upward*. Intimately. I took it, but not by choice. It was unintentional and unwelcome, yet so necessary. And providential as it had the hand of God written all over it. It was God's doing, not mine. At times, it felt like a forced march. In retrospect, it was clearly a pilgrimage. I was compelled to make the journey by the Spirit that was beyond me but who, in time, I came to realize was within me. Some might consider it a fall from grace, but I am convinced it was just the opposite: a fall into grace.

It began in earnest with quitting. I could dress it up by calling it retirement or a career transition. Though falling softer on the ears and sounding more socially acceptable, it would be a lie. The simple truth is I quit. I quit my career as a Lutheran pastor. I quit trying to please and impress others. I quit trying to live up to what others expected me to do, be, and believe. I quit striving for a standard that was impossible to achieve. I stopped

3

chasing the holy grail of success and accomplishments from which I had drunk deeply, and which I discovered was poison to my soul. I quit life as I knew it.

In my quest to satisfy others and my own ego, I had done my best to control events, people, and even God. In the end, my efforts led me to the point where my life was out of control. I couldn't do my work anymore, I couldn't do *me* anymore, I couldn't do life anymore. So I gave in and gave up. I gave up my career of almost thirty years. I gave up the faith I had practiced for most of my life. I gave up my family, at least for a time. I gave up some of those people I thought were my friends, and not so surprisingly, they gave up on me. I gave up my source of income, and because I did, I had to give up the dream house I had spent ten years pouring my heart, soul, and small pieces of my flesh into renovating and remodeling. I realized that I was the one in need of reconstruction, renewal, and resurrection. I took off my clerical collar, removed the pectoral cross that had become a weight around my shoulders and within my soul, discarded the ecclesiastical garb that had served as little more than garland to cover up my phoniness and, in truth, was simply serving to decorate the corpse of the dying man hiding underneath. I got rid of it all, and I walked away.

I did so to the surprise of some, the chagrin of others, the joyful relief of a select few. It may not have been the best way, the smart way, or the right way, but it was my way. More importantly, I am convinced it was God's way. After years spent doing, sometimes begrudgingly, what I thought I should do, what I was expected to do, and what others wanted me to do, I finally did what I believed God was leading me to do, without regard to what others would think of or say about me. And thus began my pilgrimage.

I didn't have a long-term plan or a definite direction, so I followed my heart. Like the prodigal son in the parable, I set out for a far country: Scotland. I was leaving not to escape my Father but to find Him. Believing in God had given me meaning in life; doing the business of God allowed me to make a living, but finally, I had reached a point where living felt too much like dying. I didn't know what I believed, and all of the brokering and bargaining with God had left me broken. I came to the stark realization that I didn't know what—or Whom—I was believing in and talking about. What's worse, I didn't even care. I set out on a spiritual quest in the hopes of finding—or at least rediscovering—God. And I did. Or maybe God found me.

That's one of the things God does best: find people. Sometimes, God finds us in our self-isolation, desperately wishing only to be left alone. Sometimes, God discovers us in our despair, in our helplessness, and in the heart-wrenching hopelessness of our lives. Sometimes, God seeks us out in our hiding places, be they spiritual, emotional, or physical. Sometimes, God shines light upon us as we are trying to hide in plain sight, like in the sacred sanctuaries, which far too frequently feel like sarcophagi for the spiritually dead. It is here that God unearths the dying among the living, the lost among those who claim to be found, and the battered and broken who are pretending to be whole. It is here in sacrosanct buildings that people lose God, faith, and themselves. Even those who pretend to be in a relationship with God can be total strangers to the One whose word and will they claim to know so well. It is here, in the church, that I believe, yes, am convinced, I lost God. I'm just as positive about where God found me: Iona.

I know where, but I'm still not sure why. Maybe God found me because I stopped hiding behind the carefully constructed cloak of a clergyman. Maybe God found me because I was worn out from waging spiritual, emotional, and psychological warfare against the adversaries I encountered without and the demons I battled within. Maybe God found me because I was too tired to run or fight anymore and just gave up. Or maybe God found me simply because that's what God does best. God makes it a habit of finding people in the place where we're best at hiding, inside ourselves.

That's what this story is about. It is a story for anyone who has had it all and yet had nothing. It is a story that belongs to everyone who has climbed the stairs of success only to discover there's nothing meaningful at the top; who has ascended the mountain of personal achievement, only to view the dark valleys that lay beyond. It's a story for anyone who has experienced a downward spiral, a life crisis, a crash-and-burn, or who has reached the end of their rope. It is a story for those who are dying inside, desperate to live again. It is a story about death and resurrection, experienced not at some point in the future, but in the eternal moments of today.

It is a story that could apply to anyone but is especially pertinent for pastors, their spouses and children, who are the ones who too often silently suffer. It may also address the people who devotedly populate the pews on Sunday morning with their bodies while their hearts, minds, and spirits are still seeking to be spiritually fed. It is a story for people who walked out of the church doors vowing never to return, convinced that God had walked out on them. People who stopped believing in a loving God and are under the erroneous impression that God no longer loves them. It could be anyone's story, but if you're reading this, it just might be yours.

For me, it is the story of a journey that had its inception years before I ever embarked on it. My pilgrimage marked the end of one life and the beginning of another. It was a pivotal point in my life, the culmination of all the years leading up to it, and the springboard that launched me into all the years that would follow. It was ten short weeks spent on the holy isle of Iona. Before I arrived, it felt like I was only trying to escape. It didn't take long for me to feel something much different: the loving embrace of others, and God. I experienced the holy, healing, ethereal hands of God reaching out to hold me. I left all that I had set my heart on, and felt my heart begin to beat again as it received love in the most unexpected ways from some of the most unlikely and unique people I'd ever met. When I left Iona, I left a piece of my heart on that rocky outcropping. Geographically, it was a journey that took me to the heart of Scotland; spiritually, it was a journey that took me to the very heart of God, where I would find my own heart.

This book is about that journey. My purpose in writing is not simply to retell my story, but to inspire you, dear fellow pilgrim, to find a greater appreciation for the journey that you are on, or to encourage you to embark upon a new one. Perhaps, if you haven't already, you will, and in the process, find your heart, your soul, your real self, and your loving God. Or maybe, just maybe, your God will find you.

"A few places in the world are held to be holy, because of the love that consecrates them, and the faith which enshrines them. One such place is Iona…It is but a small isle, fashioned of a little sand, a few grasses salted with the spray of an ever-restless wave, a few rocks that wade in heather, and upon whose brows the sea-wind weaves their yellow lichen. But since the remotest days, sacrosanct men have bowed here in worship. In this little island a lamp was lit that lighted pagan Europe. From age to age, lowly hearts have never ceased to bring their burdens here. And here, hope waits. To tell the story of Iona is to go back to God and to end in God."[1]

---

1 Fiona MacLeod, quoted from Celtic Daily Prayer: Prayers and Readings from the Northumbria Community (HarperOne, 2002), 473.

Part One

LOSING FAITH

ONE

The Decision

THE MYSTERY OF GOD'S PRESENCE CAN ONLY BE TOUCHED
BY A DEEP AWARENESS OF GOD'S ABSENCE.
—Henry Nouwen, *The Inner Voice of Love*

I woke up that frigid January morning to another snowy, overcast day in northern Colorado. The weather mirrored my mood. The cold matched my condition. My soul was frozen, my spirit iced over. My body was dry and brittle, like the branches I peered at on the trees outside the window. I had lost weight. My skin was sallow. A friend would say later that she thought I had cancer.

Forcing myself out of bed, I began to perform the perfunctory duties to start the day. Still in a stupor, I moved through the motions of making the coffee, showering, and getting dressed. My outfit was the same one I wore most days: black pants and a matching black clerical collar. On this day, it seemed especially tight around my neck. At least I didn't have to put any thought or effort into choosing my wardrobe.

My house was empty. I say *house*, not home, because that was what it had become, simply a structure where I ate and slept. A wayside for a weary traveler. It once was a home filled with love and laughter by my wife and four daughters. But each of them had stepped out, one by one, into the new lives that awaited them. The absence of my wife Pam was a result of our sudden divorce. I was left behind to try and craft my new life in a place and profession I no longer cared about. This was a new experience, living alone, though *living* would be a generous term. More like existing. Over three thousand square feet—a home that had easily housed six had now become more like a warehouse for one. It was akin to living in a museum. I rattled and brattled around, doing my best to fill space and time with something meaningful. I was kept company by the furniture, photos, and fixtures that once added to the warm décor of this old farmhouse, but now served only as cruel reminders of a past that no longer was, and never would be again. On the surface, it still all looked good, but underneath the appearances, it was empty, like its owner. The joy, the laughter, the love that had once filled this space had made a hasty exit along with my family and been replaced by a deafening silence that became an unwelcome companion and served as a constant reminder of how meaningless my life had become.

In the same way my family had departed, so too had my calling. Oh, I was still functioning as a minister, but the enthusiasm had long since vacated my soul. My spirit was no longer willing, and my flesh was weak. Twenty-seven years serving as a pastor had taken its toll, and the youthful zeal that I first experienced as a well-educated, newly ordained neophyte was long gone. Gradually, the idealism of becoming a conqueror for Christ had been whittled away and worn down, so rather than trying to save others, I was merely trying to salvage what little I had left of myself. The beliefs that had been so carefully crafted, mostly by others, and bought into by me, had been abandoned. I felt as if I had sold my soul somewhere along the way, compromised what I believed and held most dear so that I could fit myself into the faith that I was taught was true, and meet the expectations of others and God. The pastoral persona that was on parade publicly was a façade. It wasn't who I was, and I knew it. But I had to keep others from knowing. Like the Wizard of Oz, I hid behind a curtain meant to mislead and make others think I really was something great, that I really did know God, and that I fully bought into the beliefs that I was being paid to promote. It was all smoke and mirrors, divine deception, a perfunctory performance by a pastor who had long ago lost his first love, abandoned the faith he had been taught but now felt so phony, and was only pretending to be the pastoral person that people thought, wished, and wanted him to be. The truth is I was broken.

The downward spiral that led me to this place of desolation had been gradual, at least at first. In fact, it was unnoticeable to those peering in from the outside. Externally, I was climbing the church version of Jacob's ladder of success, an all-too-common condition among clergy. I had moved from one ministry setting to another, each a bit more noteworthy, prestigious, and—of course—better-paying. The last parish had appeared to be everything I ever desired: more members, multiple staff, and a beautiful area to live in with improved educational opportunities for both my daughters and wife. But the problems had begun almost immediately after my arrival, and the descent into this deserted place that I now found myself in had rapidly accelerated. I had been constantly assailed by contentious members of the congregation and conflicts that were waiting for me before I arrived or that I had unintentionally helped to create. There were unusual, unexpected, and previously unexperienced trials faced by my daughters, such as car accidents, the deaths of classmates, and debilitating sports injuries. There were escalating pressures within my marriage due not only to the crap I carried home from the congregation but also the ongoing demands of remodeling the one-hundred-year-old farmhouse I had insisted on purchasing. Added to all of this was the fallout in my extended family from my mother having dementia. I battled the host arrayed against me, fighting on numerous fronts, trying to stay afloat and steady the ship of my life that was filling with water faster than I could bail it out and was rapidly sinking. Failure was not an option.

I had always been successful. In my previous parish, it was as if I had the Midas touch, seemingly being able to do no wrong. During those times I faced adversity, I relied on the advice and example of my father, a veteran of WWII, to "man up," to be strong, to not let others see you as weak or struggling. Giving up or surrendering was simply not an option. I had been taught by the church that great men of faith always stood tall in the face of life's storms. The call of Christ was to carry the cross. This formula had worked in the crime-ridden inner-city neighborhood in my first congregation in Chicago. This formula had worked in the jungles of Papua New Guinea. This formula had worked in the face of opposition and discord in other congregations. Or so I believed. Maybe. Or maybe not. Maybe it worked as a placebo for too long a time. Or maybe it had never worked at all. Maybe that's why I now felt so helpless, hopeless, and ready to give up. On God. On ministry. On myself. On life. After all, I was merely going through the motions of what I thought it meant for a man posing as a preacher and pretending to have a solid faith foundation. It was a poor pastoral and personal performance, a survival mechanism. I was biding my time, waiting for the final act and the final curtain to fall. On that cold, gray, Monday morning, it did.

I wanted to spend the day sequestered in solitude. Nonetheless, my pastoral duties were calling. First on my to-do list was a coffee meeting with a twenty-year-old congregation member whose parents were divorcing. He was about the same age as my youngest daughter. Sitting at that table with him was like being with one of my daughters, each of whom had been seriously affected by my own divorce four years earlier. Some believe that the severing of a marriage is easier if the children are older. Nothing could be further from the truth. Just the opposite, in fact. Older children have had years living in at least the illusion of stability, and so when parents split, it is a seismic shock that sends tremors and causes permanent damage. The divorce affected each of my daughters in unique ways. The oldest, Katie, was married and living in California. It caused her to question the effect it would have on her marriage and the example being set. Molley, the youngest, was entering her senior year in high school. That meant her last year was spent living in the maelstrom of a broken home, trying to find some sense of calm within the storm. Not only was she tasked with navigating her last year in high school without her parents' emotional stability and availability, but also to try and find solid footing from which to take the next step in her life. Kayleen and Meghan, the middle two, were both attending the same college and perhaps were able to find some comfort and consolation by clinging to each other. It was hard on each of them in ways I can't even imagine.

I was brought back to the present moment with this young man by the tears running softly down his cheeks. I saw my own four daughters' faces, the tears they had shed, the fear and resentment they felt as we did to them what this young man's parents were doing to him. As I looked at him I saw their faces; as I listened to him, I heard questions similar to those my daughters had been asking.

"Why are they doing this? Christians are supposed to forgive."

"What about the love of God that they're always talking about?"

"I don't understand how they could be so selfish. It's like they haven't even considered how this will affect me."

Painfully honest questions that couldn't and wouldn't be answered.

It was as if I had been transported back in time and was again reexperiencing the raw emotions of my divorce and reliving how it had affected my family and me. Perhaps as a coping mechanism, I went numb as he poured out his frustration, anger, and helplessness. In the past, I would have moved into a pastoral counseling mode, pretending that God had given me an answer for the problem, and then providing what I believed to be the divine recipe that would rectify or resolve the issue, or at least make the person feel better. Providing answers and trying to fix people was a disastrous and damaging default mechanism I had learned in the church. It's a behavior many overly pious religious people practice. Parroting some phrase, cliché, or Bible verse, too often lacking any real empathy or any kind of understanding in the delivery of it, in the mistaken hope that words can somehow fix the person or problem and make everything better. I had been on the receiving end of such tactics and learned from personal experience that it just didn't work. I had failed too many times trying to fix others. My God, I couldn't even fix myself! What did I have to offer him? Nothing. Not even a prayer. I had concluded that those didn't work either, no matter how devout or desperate one might be. I just sat there with him and did my best to be present in his pain without revealing that it wasn't his I was feeling, but my own.

I left the coffee shop wrung out. Feeling zombie-like, I mechanically shuffled to my car. I had another appointment waiting for me. It was a church service at a local nursing home. In the past, I had enjoyed these occasions and relished the idea of providing spiritual encouragement and giving my time and attention to the residents. It was one of the few times I could muster genuine compassion for others, even in my emotionally empty condition. Too often, they were ignored by their families and placed on a shelf like the canned goods that used to populate my parents' basement pantry. I suspect that doing such services for the aged and infirm also provided some kind of therapeutic salve for me, as the residents vicariously took the place of my dead mother.

After an eleven-year journey into the darkest depths of dementia, Mom had died three years earlier from Alzheimer's. Her disease had considerable residual effects on the family. It had nearly ruined the previously close relationship I had with my sisters, contributed to the fraying and further breakdown of my marriage, and made me seriously question the grace and goodness of God. "How could a loving God allow such a wonderful woman to suffer from such a horrible disease?" Personally, I was racked with guilt and regrets. I had failed Mom in her time of need. The opportunity had come shortly after her diagnosis to move back to Wisconsin where she lived. Instead, I selfishly grabbed the bright, shiny object that appeared to be a better pastoral position in Colorado. As the disease continued to gradually steal pieces of Mom bit by bit, I realized my mistake. I was filled with regret for not having moved back to be with her in her hour of need. I compensated for the immense guilt I felt by giving in to resentment toward others and suffocating shame for myself. I was her only son and therefore responsible for her well-being. Dad had entrusted her to me before he died so many years before. I had let both down. The lonely descent into dementia was made even worse for her, if that were possible, by my far too infrequent trips back to be with her. Subconsciously, I suspect my pastoral visits and services at assisted living facilities and memory care units were attempts to atone for my sins against my mother by doing for them what I wasn't doing for her.

The people living in care communities are keepers of a wealth of wisdom, stewards of a world of life experiences. Too often, they have no one to share them with. Other than their caregivers, very few people want to spend time with these wise ones; to listen, look at, or even touch them. During my visits, I did my best to do all three, at least with a few. Like the frontier clergy of old who would ride a circuit to provide services for numerous congregations, I visited several of these communities on a regular basis. The place I went to that Monday morning had been one of my favorites. But not that day. I didn't want to be there, or anywhere for that matter. I had nothing to give. I went through the motions, singing some old favorite religious songs, repeating the same readings, and regurgitating the same sermon that I had delivered the day before.

As I preached to these dear people of God, the guilt began to creep in again. It had become my closest companion as of late—self-imposed guilt that too often turned into shame. The church that I had known and grown up in excelled at honing the skill of self-loathing. Throughout my life, my church tradition made me aware repeatedly that I could never be good enough, no matter how hard I tried. I had come to believe that the sins that I had committed (most merely the result of being human) had made me more despicable in God's eyes. On any given day, circumstances would reveal a specific sin that caused me to wallow in self-pity and despair. On this day, the situation led me to conclude that I was cheating on God because I didn't even know if I believed the pious words I was proclaiming. I was also cheating on God's people, who assumed the person standing in front of them shared what they believed.

Somehow, I sensed that they could see right through me. I was certain that these dear old souls who knew God so well, some with cataracts, others near closing their eyes for the last time, recognized a man merely going through the motions and posing as a pastor. But in their kindness, they didn't say so. They didn't tell me what their intuitive spirits must've been telling them. They sat there, smiling throughout my sermon, and thanked me when it was over. And I thanked God also that it was over! I couldn't wait to run away and get back to my office. I was putting on my long brown dress coat, similar to the one my father used to wear, a gift I had received from my oldest daughter Katie that Christmas, and hurrying to escape when I heard the words I'd come to dread.

"Pastor, do you have a minute?"

I turned to fix my gaze on the interloper who was presenting an obstacle to my departure. She was about my age. I had seen her in the chapel, sitting beside a much older woman in a wheelchair.

"Thank you for your message. My mother and I don't have a church or a pastor, but I'm wondering if you'd mind spending some time speaking with us. We would both appreciate it."

Couldn't she sense that I didn't want to be bothered? Couldn't she see the fatigue etched on my face? As far as I was concerned, the play had ended, and I was offstage. I was finished with this performance. Didn't she know that I didn't have anyone to listen to me? Couldn't she tell that I was an empty vessel myself? Didn't she realize that I also didn't have a church or a pastor? Didn't she care that I had given all I had to offer, that there was nothing left, that the well was dry, that I was dying inside?

When you're a pastor, you're expected to keep giving, even if you have nothing left. Too much is never enough. On this occasion, that's what I did: I gave them everything I had left, which was nothing. I went with the two women, sat with them, and pretended to care as I listened to them pour out their pains, both physical and spiritual. And when they were finished, I read a Bible passage and provided what must've been a poor imitation of praying. Then I left them, hoping that God wouldn't.

As I walked out to my car, I noticed a message had been left on my cell phone. "Pastor, I need to speak with you. Don and I are having some serious issues in our marriage, and I'm wondering if you would meet with us to talk about them?" I didn't want to call her back, but I did. I probably just wanted to get it over and done with. Throughout the fifteen minutes it took to drive back to the church, I listened as she went into detail, mostly about how her husband was failing her. How was I to help? Who was I to help? I was also a husband who had failed his wife.

After twenty-five years Pam had decided she'd had enough. Added to the normal strains of marriage was the additional stress of being a pastor's wife. Though we had entered the seminary as newlyweds, there was no way she could prepare for the pressure of being married to a pastor. The expectations placed on her to be involved with parish activities paled in comparison to the those of how she should act, dress, and even mother our children. The opinions held by people in the congregation were at times expressed openly, but more often as gossip or passive aggressively. Little did people realize what a pressure cooker pastoral ministry is. It's no wonder so many clergy have marital and mental health issues, or simply give up altogether.

Though it sounds cliché, I didn't see the divorce coming. I believed that despite the difficulties we had experienced in our marriage, they were normal, and our relationship was on solid ground. I believed that marriage was for life. My parents modeled that. I thought that vows made at an altar were binding. I trusted she was in it for better or worse, faithful even unto death. I thought that I had been a good husband. I was convinced that the one person I could trust was her. Maybe all of that caused me to ignore the warning signs that must've been there.

It happened fast, in less than a year, leaving me to question much of what I believed not only about marriage, but about God. I felt deceived by her and by God. I felt that God was letting me down. I believed that I had done everything that God demanded of me, maybe even more. I was angry at God. I felt that I had done my part, but God hadn't done His. It was divine deception and betrayal, leaving me to question all that I had been so convinced of before. I thought, "How could the God that I had so ardently devoted my life to allow this to befall me?" It was a traumatic experience, portions of which I would relive every time someone mentioned divorce. That's what happened on the drive back to the office on that Monday morning.

The voice of the woman called me out of my troubled past into what felt at the time like an even more troubling present. I tried to listen, but my thoughts were self-centered. Did this woman really believe I knew how to navigate her marriage when I had done such a miserable job on my own? Or didn't she care? Did she only want someone to listen to her lamentations? If so, she had called the wrong person because I wasn't listening to her. It didn't matter to me. It really didn't. All that mattered was concluding the phone call and finding sanctuary.

"I'm sorry but I'm back at the office and have some things waiting for me." A blatant lie, "So why don't you talk to Don and get back to me about meeting together?" Click. The sad thing is that I didn't even feel bad about cutting her off.

As I walked into my office, I was suddenly overcome with a sense of dread and impending doom. I had forgotten that tonight was the first church council meeting of the new year. Of all the pastoral tasks that I abhorred, this was at the top of the list. Most meetings were spent wrangling about money and other aspects of running the church in a manner that had to do more with a business than a ministry. I closed the door to my office, turned on my computer, and mindlessly scrolled through the emails that awaited me. Most were church-related, regular, mundane stuff. However, one in particular caught my eye. As I opened and began to scan it, I slowed down and examined it more carefully. I couldn't believe what I was reading.

"Dear Mr. Patrick, we are pleased to inform you that you have been accepted as a volunteer at the Iona Community for ten weeks beginning May 5." There were more details, but that was all I needed to read. I was shocked! The demands of Christmas and the ensuing ennui that I was experiencing had erased from my memory the application I had sent in November for this position. I read it again, and again, and again. The shock was replaced by exultation. The gray clouds which had been covering me cleared, and my cold spirit began to warm. Easter had come early. It was a personal resurrection moment! My heart pounded. The sun seemed to be shining dispelling the darkness that had descended upon me. My sadness had turned to gladness! Garments of salvation had replaced my sackcloth and ashes. My prison sentence was commuted, and my parole papers had arrived! God had delivered me. I was smiling, then laughing, then crying with joy. It was as close as I'll ever come to a rapture.

I don't know how long I spent rejoicing in the news and relishing the new possibilities, but after a time, my pastoral instinct kicked in; I knew that I should pray about it to determine if this was God's will and work. I dropped to my knees, closed my eyes, and was filled with absolute clarity. I didn't need to spend more time in a pose that felt like pious pretense. I was going to Iona!

Getting up, I sat back down at my computer and wrote the following:

To: Church Council
From: Pastor Patrick

Greetings,

After the November Voter's meeting, I made an application to
serve as a volunteer with the Iona Community on the Isle of
Iona in Scotland. Today, I received notification that I have been
accepted for a period of ten weeks, beginning May 6–July 14.
I had contemplated a sabbatical leave in the past; however, I
believe it is perhaps in the best interest of the congregation to
simply grant me a peaceful release from my Call here. I would
plan on serving through confirmation Sunday in April. This
would need to be approved by the congregation as well as the
council. Thank you for your kind attention to this matter.

Peace,

Pastor

I emailed the council president when I finished writing and did not
attend the meeting that night. Contemplation and initial preparation for
my escape needed to take precedence.

In retrospect, it may have been an irresponsible and impulsive action
to take in my emotional and spiritual state. At times, I've questioned the
wisdom of what, on the surface, appears to be a knee-jerk reaction. Had I
taken more time and thought it out, I could've come up with other options,
like requesting a sabbatical of three or even six months, giving me time to
get the rest and recovery I needed. Perhaps it would've given me a different perspective on my ministry and my life. But at the time, there was no
choice; all I could think of was leaving and returning to the place where
I had once felt most alive, where my soul felt at home: Iona. Like a muse,
the holy isle was singing an enchanting song for me to come to her. I could
hear her soothing voice, inviting me to settle into the solitude of the sacred
isle, to step gently back into her primeval beauty, to breathe in the salty

sea air and the restorative breath of her Holy Spirit that hovered over its waters. Was I running from my problems? Yes. And subconsciously from the person I had become and no longer recognized or wanted to be. I was running from the darkness that had taken up residence with me, and from the shadow of the small self I had become. More importantly, and this I knew full well, I was also running *towards* something: the hope of finding a new life, the authentic me that I had lost so long ago, and the real God, whom I had abandoned somewhere along the way. As I sat in my office, I began to reflect on the arduous journey that had brought me to this place.

TWO

Disillusionment

AM FEAR A THE'ID A DH'L, THEID E TRI' UAIREAN ANN.
—Celtic Saying, which means,
"Those who come to Iona will come not once, but three times."

The first step onto Iona, fourteen years earlier, felt sacred. I had looked at it from afar in photos and envisioned it in my mind's eye based on descriptions I'd read. A few minutes before, I had seen it much closer as I waited at Fionnphort, the last outpost on the Isle of Mull that served as the threshold to the Holy Island. There, with my family, I boarded the ferry that would take me across the sound and complete the last leg of my journey to this holy destination.

Though my body was chilled from the wind whipping across the deck and the cold Scotland rain that was falling, my heart was warm as I stood on the upper deck eagerly peering across the bay, filled with anticipation and unbridled enthusiasm. There she was, the one who would become the love of my life, waiting to welcome me. I could feel her arms stretching out to me, inviting me to melt into her warm embrace. The ancient rocks jutted from the land, rising towards the heavens as the wind whistled, quietly playing a soft tune on this hallowed ground. The small fishing boats, some brightly colored blue, red, and yellow, bobbing rhythmically near the quay seemed to be waving a well-choreographed welcome. The quaint village comprised perhaps two hundred permanent inhabitants of small stone homes neatly aligned in a queue as if awaiting the arriving guests upon whom they would heap Celtic hospitality. Lush green pastures enclosed by stone walls invited the weary pilgrim to take refuge among the white sheep contentedly grazing. Standing watch over this heavenly landscape was the Abbey. Rebuilt from remnants and earlier ruins of other historic buildings, it appeared like a fortress, a citadel of ancient faith, standing watch like a sentinel, casting a loving eye on all who would enter this holy habitation.

Though it took only a few minutes, this last part of the trip seemed to last forever. After what seemed an eternity, the huge ramp was lowered, and the ferry disgorged its human cargo. Overwhelmed in heart and spirit, I felt like leaping, jumping, and running from the jetty. Restraining myself, I slowly and deliberately took the first step to a place that would one day lead to an exhilarating new life. Stepping aside so others could pass by me. I stopped and stood still, mesmerized momentarily not only by the sight but also by the feel of the place. Aside from the sound of the ferry and the waves breaking against the shore, it was so quiet and peaceful. There was a sense of comfort and coziness, like wearing a warm sweater made of sheep wool, a common commodity here. I stood there, trying my best to allow my soul to soak it all in. My moment of mindfulness was disrupted by the excited voices of my children cajoling me to catch up. They were excited also, frolicking ahead like little lambs, peering excitedly into the windows of a few small shops. The souvenirs caught their eager eyes, as did the clothing items and other trinkets on display. Moving quickly past the shops and up the small hill, we arrived at the remnant of old walls, marking the ruins of the ancient nunnery. Standing there, I experienced the sad solemnity of the lives of the many women who had once found refuge here. I sensed that even my family felt it. All was quiet around us. Not a menacing or eerie silence, but a comforting one. It was as if the voices of those faithful women long since departed, women who had for too long been silenced, were still whispering. As we moved through the ruins, I realized I was feeling something I hadn't experienced for a long time: serenity.

As we exited the ruins of the nunnery, I felt filled with awe and overcome with admiration for those who had walked before us and whose spirits were leading us down this path now. The path led past well-groomed gardens, the lone elementary school on the island, the small Scottish church, the

St. Columba Hotel, a jewelry store, and other small shops. What captured my attention and caused me to pause was a small stone building with a bright green door, inexplicably inviting me to come closer. I obeyed the call and drew near. For some reason I stood before it transfixed, as if in a trance. This small green door seemed to have some sort of magical power, drawing me closer and inviting me in. Perhaps it was merely my imagination, stirred by the Celtic myths I had read. Or maybe it really was some sort of a gateway capable of transporting travelers like me into a different, more transcendent reality. Whatever it was, I allowed myself to be carried along, conducted back through time to the beginning of the journey embarked upon many years before that had brought me to this sacred moment in time and space.

My pastoral ministry began upon my graduation from the seminary and ordination in 1988. I was a twenty-six-year-old, wet-behind-the ears, thoroughly indoctrinated and infatuated with God, ready-to-conquer-the world, far too full of myself, pastor. I was assigned to serve at Bethel Lutheran Church and School in Chicago, an inner-city congregation that was slowly decaying, a reflection of the surrounding neighborhood and the urban blight infecting it. Humboldt Park, once an oasis for Sunday revelers, now a haunt for gang members and drug dealers, was only blocks away. The area around Bethel had first been settled by German immigrants over one hundred years earlier. The church building was a testament to the beautiful traditional architectural style of the time. A colossal steeple rising from a roof towering three stories above the street dwarfed the surrounding dwellings. Expansive concrete steps led up to three massive wooden doors, eliciting an image of the type Luther nailed the 95 Theses, which launched the Reformation. Another set of doors separated the narthex from the sanctuary, a massive space with a running balcony which, in its heyday, could've easily held five hundred people. A red carpet, which had seen much better days, ran down the center. Ornate stained-glass windows, some pocked with bullet holes that had been duct-taped over, allowed natural light to illuminate the space. The main floor contained immense wooden pews, most of which were unoccupied even on Sundays. The organ's massive pipes rose up like slender tree trunks behind the front altar. The white marble altar was adorned with elaborate carvings and served as the focal point of the sanctuary. To the right of the altar was a large, elevated pulpit, the wood of which was ornately decorated. This was a preacher's paradise. The beauty inside this holy space starkly contrasted with the ugliness found on the streets just a few feet away. The first time I entered the church, I fell on my knees in front of the altar railing, convinced that this truly was the dwelling place of God. In truth, it was a memorial to better days long since past.

The industrious Germans who had immigrated to this part of the city were long gone. The congregation was comprised mainly of older members, former sons and daughters of the congregation who had fled the neighborhood when it began to get bad. They would faithfully drive in to attend Sunday morning service and place their generous donations in the offering plates to keep the place open. The community consisted of lower-class Latinos, African Americans, and a bevy of gangbangers. It was a strange mix. The movie *Sister Act* starring Whoopi Goldberg provides a pretty accurate picture of what it was like.

What was a country boy from Wisconsin doing in an urban jungle? This was no place for my young wife and two small daughters. No one wanted to raise their family here, including those stuck here due to their life and economic circumstances. Certainly, I reasoned, God had made a mistake. Despite my misgivings, I chose to make the best of my assignment until I could escape.

During the day, I would take time to walk the streets outside the church, picking up broken bottles and trash while greeting neighbors sitting on their front steps, some of whom were sipping beer or cheap wine far too early in the day. Making my regular rounds, I would occasionally take time to clean off the graffiti that adorned the walls of the church and school building, and if I had the time and desire, I would do the same to other nearby edifices. The parsonage in which we lived, provided at no cost to us by the congregation, sat adjacent to the church. Though it was amply equipped with sturdy locks, I nonetheless slept with a metal pipe under the bed for the first three months we lived there. Though it would've been ineffective against an intruder, it assuaged my fear, which had quickly taken up residence inside me.

Because of our close proximity to the church, part of my caretaking duties was to turn off the church alarm, which went off about one time a week. It could only be disarmed manually from inside the church; thus, when it began to blare, usually in the wee hours of the night, I would spring out of bed, grab the keys, stumble down our steps, and make my way into the eerily illuminated edifice. I would then walk quietly through the halls and classrooms of the school and into the sanctuary to ensure that a human intruder hadn't tripped it. Not once in the three years that I lived there did I encounter a living person, though, on one occasion, I did find burnt matches lying on the floor of the sanctuary. The thought of how easily those could've caused a conflagration was truly troubling.

After making the rounds, I would then wade out into the night to see who or what else might be disturbing the peace. On some nights when I was wide awake and knew that falling back to sleep was an impossibility, I would ascend an old wooden ladder into the cupola of the church and peer out, like a living gargoyle looking down on the world below. It was not unusual to see some sort of commotion being caused by the gang members who belonged to the Latin Disciples. They claimed the corner just outside the church as part of their hood and frequently hung out there at night. Occasionally, there were fights, sometimes with rival gangs, but most of the time, the activity centered around minor drug deals, cars driving by to score their nickel bag. They would sometimes shoot out the streetlights illuminating their dark lives, so the exact details of who was doing what were difficult to discern. Yet ambient lighting provided enough clarity to give me at least some sketchy details of what these lost boys were doing. In time, I came to know them by name and developed a good enough relationship with them that I would, on occasion, go to see them after they'd been incarcerated.

The traditional pastoral responsibilities of leading worship services, preaching sermons, teaching Bible classes, and visiting the sick and homebound were a given. Added to this were the daunting tasks of trying to save not only the parish but the attached parochial school. The tuition that was charged did not come near the cost of covering the expenses incurred. There were also times when I would be called to help with a domestic abuse issue in the neighborhood. And of course there was the constant challenge of dealing with the gangbangers and trying to prevent other youth from joining their ranks. To reach the at-risk youth, we would open the school classrooms and gymnasium one night a week for "Youth Night," allowing the teenagers, some of them already members of the gang, to play basketball, and the younger children to join in games and activities led by students from the nearby Lutheran college. The children and youth would, on occasion, attend a Sunday service. Two of the young men, Angel and Junito, even became confirmed members, making "the good confession" in front of the entire congregation. Nonetheless, it felt as if the considerable effort I was putting in wasn't paying off. I wasn't seeing the results I hoped for in the neighborhood, church, or school. The seminary hadn't prepared me for the difficult demands of a "non-traditional" urban parish.

Prior to my final year serving there, I had set a goal of one hundred; one hundred children in the school and an average Sunday worship attendance of one hundred as well. I exerted all my energy and ingenuity in trying to make both happen. I passed out flyers advertising the school to the neighborhood houses surrounding the church. I went door to door practically cajoling whoever answered to come to church. I became a bean counter in a clergy collar. But when the final enrollment figures were in, there were only 94 students. And the church attendance seldom topped 80. I considered it a personal failure on my part. God hadn't held up His end of the bargain either.

In addition to the considerable pastoral responsibilities, so were those of being a parent. The family was growing; our third daughter, Meghan, was born a year after our arrival. The relatively meager salary I was being paid at the time was never enough to make ends meet. Without occasional financial help from my mom and an anonymous gift from a member of the congregation, we wouldn't have stayed afloat. Three years of enduring the pressures of church, school, neighborhood, and family had stretched me beyond my abilities of pastoral skill and personal patience. I sought to escape. So I contacted a former seminary professor who had taught Missions and asked him if he could help me get another call, preferably as a missionary overseas. It didn't take long for the executive in charge of mission work for the national church organization to contact me. This man, though a pastor, was the church version of a "suit" and oversaw international mission work. He called me personally to recruit me to sign on and go overseas.

"Hi Ralph, this is Jim from the synodical mission department. I spoke with one of your seminary professors, and he urged me to contact you to see if you are interested in serving as an overseas missionary. We are in desperate need of ordained clergy like you who have an understanding of cross-cultural ministry. Would you consider serving the Lord in such a capacity?" His call gave the definite impression that I was greatly needed and a very valuable commodity, something my fragile ego badly needed to hear. He also implicitly implied that my talents could be put to better use elsewhere. There were more opportunities for overseas work than there were warm bodies willing to fill them. My somewhat damaged self-esteem due to what I perceived as some pastoral failures eagerly bought into his very effective sales pitch.

It took some time for the pieces to be put into place, during which we discovered that my wife was pregnant with our fourth child. So, when the "Divine Call" came to go to Papua New Guinea, I responded that it would be impossible. Jim would not be dissuaded and assured me there was a top-notch surgeon on the mission field who could provide for a safe delivery of our child. I felt it was a moot point, and the time wasn't right, and I told him so. During the short walk back from the church to the parsonage, I felt as if the rug had been pulled out from under me. I told my wife, Pam, about the phone call and that I had rejected the offer.

"Why?" she responded.

"Because we have three young daughters and are expecting our fourth. There's no way we can go," I replied.

To my surprise and delight, she said that she had no reservations about taking the girls over or giving birth elsewhere as long as there was a hospital and well-trained medical personnel. Perhaps her faith was greater than mine, or maybe she was even more desperate to escape our surroundings than I was. We prayed a bit and started the preparations for our departure. For two months, it was a whirlwind of activity as we sold most of our furniture and worldly goods, packed some essentials to be shipped in a container, and with our three—soon to be four—young daughters in tow, we left our friends and family to become evangelistic missionaries in the highlands of Papua New Guinea. It was a decision that would lead me to question not only my aptitude and abilities as a pastor and missionary, but also my beliefs about church and ministry that had propelled me down that path.

Meanwhile, though my family had moved on to further explore Iona, I tarried there in front of the green door, relishing the experience of remembering in greater detail the time spent in PNG and all that came after.

THREE

Distance

THE SPIRITUAL JOURNEY IS NOT A CAREER OR A SUCCESS STORY.
IT IS A SERIES OF HUMILIATIONS OF THE FALSE SELF
THAT BECOME MORE AND MORE PROFOUND.
—Thomas Keating, *An Invitation to Love*

We had no clue what awaited us. Jim at headquarters had made the work of a missionary sound romantic and described PNG in an enchanting way, evoking images in my mind's eye of the types of pictures found in *National Geographic*. Tribal people living in a pristine setting just waiting to welcome us. It almost sounded more like an adventurous vacation than a God-given calling. I was intent on proving myself and the enormity of my faith, which I privately had felt was faltering, as well as improving upon my personal sanctity. Certainly, people (though who exactly, I couldn't tell) would admire me for abandoning the comforts of the Western world, and zealously forsaking everything and almost everyone dear to me for the purpose of doing meaningful work in God's kingdom. What better place than Papua New Guinea? An island nation populated by over seven hundred tribes, some of whom had recently made the leap from the stone to the modern age. Although missionaries of all religious stripes had been present in some regions of the country for over one hundred years, I told myself that this was a people ripe for the picking, and who would appreciate the gospel message that I was eager to proclaim. The Enga Province in the Highlands, where we were being sent, had not had as much contact with Western religion as other areas, the first missionaries having arrived only forty years before. Many of the tribal members, though claiming some form of Christianity, still clung to old animistic beliefs and tribal ways. It was a syncretistic soup we were stepping into. Tribal fights and revenge murders were more the rule than the exception. The police kept the peace by burning houses and killing pigs, the most prized of all possessions. Upon our arrival, we were told that if we happened to hit a pedestrian while driving our truck and stopped to help, we'd likely be punished on the spot with an axe to the head.

The journey to PNG was relatively uneventful, which was a minor miracle, considering we were traveling with three children under the age of six, and my wife was six months pregnant. A twenty-four-hour layover in Hawaii helped make it more manageable. Upon touching down in the capital city of Port Moresby in Papua New Guinea, we were met by Barry, the mission coordinator on the field. We were hit with an almost suffocating wall of humid tropical heat as we stepped out of the airport. The intense equatorial sun had provided a shocking replacement for the cold November weather we had left behind. The city had a fortress feel, as if it was under siege. High walls, often with razor wire running the length of them, appeared to be small prison compounds protecting the homes within. The street was covered with red splotches, some of which had the hue of dried blood. Barry explained that this was the sputum of Buai, also called *betelnut*, the PNG version of chewing tobacco. It was considered a mild aphrodisiac. It was common to see both men and women with a cheek full, and the red fluid dripping down their chins.

Barry took us to a nearby restaurant with outdoor seating for lunch, treating us to burgers and fries, which served to provide a bit of familiarity in a very unfamiliar setting. It was necessary to take weekly doses of chloroquine as a prophylactic to prevent malaria. The huge and horrible-tasting pills were distributed during our tropical dining experience. Each of us did our best to choke them down. Our third oldest daughter, Meghan, only two at the time, had an especially difficult time swallowing them, so much so that she began to gag and then regurgitate it, a fitting foretaste of what was awaiting us.

After lunch finished, we returned to the airport for the short plane ride to Mt. Hagen. After arriving there, Barry loaded us into his Toyota extended cab truck, our luggage in the storage box behind the cab, for the two-hour drive to the mission station called Birip. The scenery was intoxicating. Lush mountain rainforests were pierced by waterfalls cascading off the majestic cliffs. It was as if we had touched down in Jurassic Park. The mountain roads were quite narrow, with no guard rails providing even a modicum of protection from the steep drop-offs into the valleys below. We did our best to look out and not down, but occasionally we would sneak a peek over the edge into the abyss below and hold on even more tightly for dear life. Small roadside shacks constructed from rough-cut timber with tin roofs would appear wherever there was a nearby village. These were the local version of convenience stores, serving up coke, fried flour balls, and greasy globs of fried sheep fat referred to as "lamb flaps." The most provocative sight was the people dressed in a wide variety of native garments; some women wore grass skirts with decorative shells hanging around their necks, or brightly colored skirts with floral designs called "lap laps." Some of the older women were topless, the younger ones wore black brassieres or floral smocks. Younger men wore western style trousers and T-shirts, but the older men preferred to wear a small covering made of leaves. Some of them had bones in their noses. We weren't in Chicago anymore.

We were treated upon our arrival to a small cohort of missionaries who had been eagerly awaiting our arrival. The next few days would find us settling in at our initial mission station called Amapyaka, where we would focus on language study and enculturation. Due to the fact that it was early December, we did our best to prepare our home and family for the fast-approaching Christmas holiday, and the impending birth not only of the baby Jesus, but our own baby as well. How would we make this Christmas special for our three little girls who had been uprooted from all that was familiar? All the things that had made Christmas magical in the past—snow, Christmas trees, decorations and lights—were nowhere to be found. We were bereft of the conveniences, such as grocery stores in which to buy the turkey and stuffing, as well as the extras, such as candy to fill the stockings. Our annual holiday trip to Macy's on Michigan Avenue was nothing more than a memory. Plus, there were no family members or friends. We were surrounded by strangers, both the nationals and the expats with whom we had come to live. In addition, the moving container in which we'd packed some of the amenities that might have helped us feel more at home wouldn't arrive for another two months. We made up our minds to do as best we could with the bare necessities. A diesel generator provided the station with electricity for three hours every night, so we were able to fashion a few Christmas lights that had been left by previous missionaries into the shape of a tree on our wall. The nearest town to purchase anything was Mt. Hagen, which was two hours away. But even there, the choices were severely limited. There were no canned goods for green bean casserole or pumpkin pie. One couldn't even purchase a turkey or ham. Therefore, Christmas Day found us feasting on a rather robust chicken bought for $10 from a local farmer and sweet potatoes, the staple food in Enga. Santa had managed to squirrel away a couple of small gifts that had been hidden well in separate suitcases. It was a bare-bones celebration, but the lack of accoutrements and focus on acquiring things gave it a sweet and simple feel, with attention paid to what mattered most: family and faith. It may well have been one of the most meaningful holidays we'd ever experienced.

During the days leading up to Christmas, we made it our mission to get more familiar with our surroundings, which included a day-long visit to Mambisanda, the hospital where our fourth daughter was soon to make her arrival in this strange new world. Like so much of the rest of the infrastructure in the Enga Province, the hospital had been built by missionaries about thirty years earlier. Mambisanda was a half-hour drive over a very bumpy dirt road. The prospect of traversing this while in full labor was not an attractive thought to Pam. Upon arrival, we were treated to a tour that took much longer than anticipated, due in part to the frequent pauses we would take to process the radical differences between this hospital and the ones we were familiar with at home. Lacking were the white walls, the semi-private rooms, the polished floors, and the sterile smells and appearance. Instead, we were greeted with the appalling appearance of patients all convalescing together in large wards that housed at least thirty people each. The walls were dingy and the floors dirty, evidence of years of neglect.

And the smell was indescribably unique, a mixture of smoke, body odor, pus, and lingering infections. The patients were being treated for a variety of afflictions, some of which were common to our experience, like broken bones and cancer, and others much less so, like axe and machete wounds resulting from tribal fights. There was a shortage of medical staff, and no hospital kitchen or cafeteria, so the family members themselves were expected to provide much of the care as well as the necessary nourishment for their loved ones.

After getting over the initial shock of what we were seeing, our consternation was gradually transformed into a modicum of compassion. Here before us were the people that the Great Physician had spoken of when He described His purpose as healing the brokenhearted, binding up wounds, curing the lepers and all of those with various afflictions, and proclaiming the Year of the Lord's favor. Could we, I wondered, do the same?

The feeling of compassion for these people of God was offset by my concern for Pam, as she would soon be delivering our child within these very walls. On the drive home, we talked about all that we had experienced, and to her credit, she said, "If Mary could give birth in a stable, I can give birth here." A more trusting expression of faith I have seldom heard.

Two months later, on February 17, we made the return trip to Mambisanda, where our fourth daughter, Molley, was born. The labor progressed quickly, the delivery was safe, the baby was healthy, and our three other daughters, waiting during the day at the home of the missionary doctor's house, were delighted. Of the four births, this one turned out to be perhaps the most memorable. This was due not only to the surroundings and the expertise of those attending, but also the presence of our other children. Having them there made this moment all the more special. Later that afternoon, we made the drive back to our house at Amapyaka over those same bumpy roads. Pam's strength and fortitude was so admirable, as was her patience as she convalesced in the company of her husband and now four daughters.

The ensuing four months were spent settling in, learning the culture and language, and getting acclimated to this new life with four children. Late in June, we were transferred to our permanent mission station at Yaramanda, located just across the Lai River valley, approximately five miles from Mambisanda. Yaramanda was the site of the first Lutheran mission in the Enga Valley, built by Rev. Otto Hinze, who arrived in Enga in 1948. Though he had left the field and returned to the U.S. years before we arrived, he was still somewhat of a living legend. Some of the older people, referred to as *Lapun* in Melanesian Pidgin, would still recount stories of the Hintze family. They were revered in an almost worshipful way, having set the standard for what, in the minds of the nationals, missionaries were expected to be. It was a set of expectations I would fail miserably to live up to.

The house at Yaramanda that we lived in was built by the Hintzes. It was a basic, rustic version of what in the States would be called "ranch style." It had three bedrooms, an indoor bathroom with a small square tub for bathing, and no shower. The walls were covered with a mat woven from bamboo-like material called *pit pit*. The kitchen had a wood stove for cooking. A diesel generator again provided the power to generate electricity for a few hours each day. In essence, we had stepped back at least fifty years in time.

There hadn't been a missionary family at the Yaramanda station for over ten years, so most of the people were thrilled to have us. The welcome we received was overwhelming. We felt as if we had been adopted by the tribe. They were especially taken with the three little blonde-haired girls and the new baby. They showered us with gifts of food, live chickens, *billums* (woven bags that carried everything from vegetables to infants), and even a little pig. Pigs were highly valued in the culture, being used to settle tribal fights on the one hand and purchase brides on the other.

A bride price consisted of both kina and pigs.[1] It was not only a sign of goodwill from one tribe to the other, but also an investment in the marriage. If the couple were to divorce, which was quite rare, the bride's tribe would be required to return the full price. In the event of fights that ended in serious injury or death, it was necessary to pay compensation to the members of the other tribe to make retribution for the injuries caused or redeem the life of the person.

---

1 Kina is the name of the national currency. It's based on the decorative shell found along the coast. It was commonly worn as jewelry and as a display of a person's wealth.

Without clocks to punch or places to go, life was simple. When the demands of daily life had been met, there was ample time to be with the children, bake bread, plant a garden, walk to the roadside market, and socialize as best we could with the nationals. Life was basic, sometimes hard, but very fulfilling, at least for a time.

The honeymoon period had ended by the end of our first year in the country. The difficulties of daily living had set in. There were no nearby stores where we could purchase needed supplies. Cooking on a wood stove to feed a family of six was a chore for Pam. The children frequently got head lice, and battling the biting fleas that would populate their pajamas at night was an ongoing problem. Giardia and other stomach-related illnesses that usually resulted from eating any food that wasn't prepared in our own kitchen was quite common. The romanticism we felt when we first arrived was replaced with the demands of daily life, as well as my disappointment at not having a meaningful missionary role.

What am I doing here? I often wondered. I began to believe that I had been sold a bill of goods. I began to realize that Jim had presented a glossy portfolio of the work in PNG, painting a fictitious picture that functioned as a well-crafted sales pitch to enlist a naïve recruit. He had led me to believe that I would be going to convert an animistic pagan people who were living in darkness and the shadow of eternal death. I fully bought into the fable, part of which I fabricated myself. I was taught that being a missionary was the highest form of service and sacrifice a person could make to God. It meant following in the footsteps of gospel greats like J. Hudson Taylor or Amy Carmichael. It was a fairy tale of faith that I swallowed hook, line, and sinker.

The people of Enga had already been thoroughly evangelized. At that time, PNG claimed a Christian population of 95 percent. The national church organization in Enga, the Gutnius Lutheran Church, was embroiled in a leadership conflict. Two sides were battling for control of the meager financial resources still being sent from the church organization back in the U.S. There was an abundance of trained national clergy who were more than capable of continuing the work being done there. The moniker of *missionary*, as I understood it, was a misnomer. There were more unbelievers in the place I had just left than in PNG. I gradually came to believe that I had not been sent there by God but by men like Jim to prop up the leadership and ensure that the flow of money being sent was being properly spent. I felt like I was seen as a cash cow by the national clergy, someone whose main purpose was to help keep the money supply flowing. It was a refined welfare system meant to maintain control over dependent people who were told that this was part of the divine plan for church structure. As my eyes began to open, my heart began to close. I felt deceived. The spiritual cataracts began to blind me, and I began to distance myself not only from faith in the organization that had sent me there, but also faith in the God who I felt was ultimately responsible. I was filled with doubts and began to seriously question my faith in a loving God. These doubts continued to build up, opening the door to discouragement and disillusionment.

I attempted to arrest the process by assuaging my conscience with gospel "self-talk," selling myself on the idea that I had done what Jesus commanded: take up my cross to follow him, leave family, and go into the world to make disciples of all nations. But even I wasn't buying the product I was peddling. The harder I tried to convince myself of the sanctity of the mission, the more evident it became that I had been duped. I felt like a fool for dragging my family with me on what I saw as a fiasco.

Still, I held out hope for the situation to improve. The new school term at the Bible school where I would be teaching was scheduled to begin in January. It would be my job to oversee two teachers and approximately fifteen students. The students received one year of basic theological training. Upon successful completion of the program, some would return to their tribes to serve as evangelists, and others who had shown a significant aptitude for their studies would go on to the seminary. The literacy capabilities of the students were equivalent to perhaps a third- or fourth-grade level in the U.S. Therefore, the curriculum was very basic, consisting of simple lessons covering Old and New Testament stories, and the most fundamental doctrines of the Lutheran church.

There were two national pastors with whom I would be working, Reseti and Kambu. Kambu had been an early convert to Christianity and had been elevated to the role of teacher because of his experience. Reseti was younger, closer to my age, a seminary graduate who was quite adept theologically. Together, the three of us prepared by acquiring supplies, cleaning the classroom, and deciding how to divide the teaching responsibilities.

The students gradually began to arrive at the Bible school and get settled into their rudimentary dormitory housing. It was no small thing for students to leave their tribal homes to live and study in a different location. The tribe was their safety and security. Loyalty to the tribe and the tribe's loyalty to them meant everything. To leave one's tribe was to expose oneself to an unknown and potentially very dangerous situation. It was a mark of great faith for them to embark on this journey.

The excitement on the first day of class was palpable, not only for the students and teachers, but for me as well. I had been in the country for over a year, and finally, I would be doing something significant other than learning the language and familiarizing myself with the culture. Though not exactly what I expected, at least I had a sense of purpose again. Perhaps this is what I had come here for, to teach and help prepare men to do what I considered the real work of God.

We had just finished our introductions and distribution of books and materials when there was a knock at the door. I assumed it was a late-arriving student that hadn't been accounted for. Instead, it was the leader of a local tribe, called an *Akali Komongo*, which means "big man," a title given to those who had accumulated wealth and power, reflected in their multiple wives, property, and pigs. Indeed, he was a very large man, standing almost six feet tall and weighing close to three hundred pounds. His girth was also evidence of his wealth, for in a culture whose staple food was the sweet potato, only those who had ample means to purchase an abundance of food could be so fat. As I stepped out of the classroom, I was met with a vitriolic verbal barrage delivered in a combination of Engan, Pidgin, and broken English.

"You cannot meet here. You must close immediately. The students must all leave. And you must leave also."

Kambu and Reseti served as translators in order to ensure that I didn't misunderstand his message. I stood there shell-shocked for what seemed like an eternity, but in reality, it was most likely a few moments. In time,

I discovered that this man was a supporter of the pastor who claimed to be the legitimate bishop of the church and who was fighting to regain his ecclesiastical power. In addition, there was an ongoing conflict between the three local tribes, the Wauni, Maini, and Pyapini, all of which bordered the Bible school property. Originally it was the site of the large field that served as the battleground site for the three tribes. Hintze and the first missionaries intended to convert the land from a place of hatred to one of peace. It had worked for a while, but after a time each of the tribes laid claim to the land where the Bible school was located, primarily for the purpose of receiving the rent money the church in America paid to have the Bible school located there.

My fear gave way to anger, and I began to fume at this untimely and unwelcome affront. The assault fueled my previous frustrations that had been building up during the past year, and suddenly, they began to pour out.

"You may be a big man in your tribe, but you have no authority here," I yelled at him. "This school, and this land, was given to God and belongs to Him. I am here to serve God and these students, not you."

I expected my response to have the same kind of effect that confronting a barking dog has. I thought he would back down and leave, but instead, he responded even more aggressively. "That may be so, but if you don't close the school, I will burn your house down and kill your family."

I had been a witness to acts of violence in Chicago, but never had I been personally threatened by it. In retrospect, it is likely that these were mere threats, and the man was probably only trying to frighten me. Nonetheless, at that moment, it was extremely unsettling, not only for me but also for Reseti, Kambu, and the students, all of whom had witnessed the entire altercation. For them, it was more than a threat, for they had been part of tribal wars, no doubt perpetrators as well as victims of the violence. Without their tribe, they were vulnerable and made for easy targets. The intruder turned and began to walk away, but as he did so, he reiterated his threat, "Close the school, or I will set a trap for your truck and kill your family."

Badly shaken, we retreated into the classroom to discuss what had just transpired. To a man, the students all wanted to return to the safety of their own tribes. Regardless of what I decided, the students had made up their minds to leave. And so, on the very day classes started, the school closed, and everyone returned home. I retreated to my house on the hill like a beaten dog with its tail between its legs. I was furious, shaken, and afraid.

Fear is like a cancer that slowly eats away at a person. It starts small, hardly detectable, but if left untreated, it slowly metastasizes and eventually sucks the life from the host. This is what was happening to me. The darkness that had begun to lurk in the Chicago street shadows had followed me to this wild tropical frontier half a world away. The setting couldn't have been more different: an urban jungle on the one hand and a tropical jungle on the other. Gangs gathered with guns on street corners in Chicago, and tribes engaged in warfare with weapons like spears and axes on the other. Those fears weren't necessarily irrational, as I watched firsthand from the church cupola in Chicago. It's just that now it had become personal. I was now the target, along with my family. I was responsible for any harm that would come to my wife and four beautiful daughters. All the Bible passages I could muster to try and bolster my failing faith weren't enough to dispel the complete lack of courage and the impotency that I was feeling. In time, it would permeate what I had thought were the impenetrable walls of my own self confidence and trust in God.

As I sat in my house licking my wounds, I chastised myself for my pride and arrogance. I had made a move that was irrational and irresponsible. Why, if I had to leave Chicago, didn't I go back to Wisconsin to be closer to Mom, still grieving the death of Dad just a few years earlier? Why did I feel compelled to do something out of the ordinary, some great exercise of faith hoping to impress others and God? Why did I intentionally subject my cherished children and wonderful wife to danger and possible death in a dark place at the hands of a people I was quickly coming to despise?

The religious refrain of "fear not" that I had heard repeated so frequently in scripture and had piously proclaimed to other people from the pulpit had fallen impotently upon my own deaf ears and distraught spirit. In the days and weeks that followed, this inchoate fear had begun to grow, taking on the form of guilt and shame. I began to suffer the full effects of this insidious process. Emotionally, I became resentful and angry, a simmering pot that would, at times, boil over, burning those whom I loved the most. I became difficult to live with, frequently lashing out verbally at my wife for small mishaps and minor mistakes, all of which I blamed on her. I would reprimand my daughters for laughing too loudly for my liking or turn small infractions common to little kids into major violations. I clearly recall my wife doing her best to encourage me, trying her best to get me to see events from a different perspective. At times, she even pleaded with me to find a different purpose there, like spending my ample free time, now that the school was closed, mastering the native language to translate the Old Testament, or to spend more time and effort reaching out to the tribes in more isolated areas. I refused. It was then, I am convinced, that the distance between us began to widen, and the seeds of discontent that led to our divorce eighteen years later began to grow. I plowed the soil with my discouragement, planted it with despondency, watered it with despair, and watched it blossom into depression. It was an introduction to an acquaintance who would make more appearances in the future. It would only take time, and more ministry disappointments, for it to fully bloom.

It was almost as if I relished reveling in the doldrums. I became argumentative with colleagues, at times refusing to participate in important events. On one occasion, I boycotted the seminary graduation. Being moved to another mission station after a year didn't help. It served only as a reminder of my failure and put an exclamation point on the fact that my original purpose was beyond saving. And maybe, I wondered, so was I.

December of 1994 marked the end of our three-year commitment and couldn't arrive fast enough for me. Though it was difficult for my wife and daughters to bid farewell to their close friends who had become like family, it didn't affect me in the same way. I was anxious to leave this place that symbolized all that was wrong with missions, the church, and me. I hoped that by saying goodbye to this inferno that had become my personal hell, I would also be able to bid farewell to the unfamiliar man that I had become. In time, I would learn that wherever one goes; one must take themselves with them. It would be a hard lesson.

Our return trip took us first to Australia, where we spent a week visiting friends who had formerly lived in Enga. It provided a soft landing, especially for the children, as they were introduced back into the culture they had come from, but which now seemed like a stranger. Stores stocked with every item imaginable, McDonald's and other fast-food restaurants, and no longer needing to fight fleas or get sick with giardia provided immense delight for all of us. After a week spent in transition, we boarded the flight from Sydney for the long flight home. Stepping off the plane in Minnesota, we were greeted by a large contingent of relatives waiting at the gate to meet us. Those were the days before tight airport security when people were allowed to traverse airports at will. They gave us a hero's welcome home, and the warm embrace of my sisters, and especially my mom, was immensely comforting and helped to soothe the sense that not only were the last three years a complete failure, but so was I.

We spent six months of furlough time living with my widowed mother, Jean, in her home in northern Wisconsin. My father had died seven years earlier, and she had spent much of the time since living in long stretches of solitude, social isolation, and loneliness, all of which was compounded by a grief that she described as "something you never get over, but just learn to live with." She would, on occasion, refer to her living situation as solitary confinement. Thus, she was ecstatic to have her only son, her daughter-in-law whom she adored, and four delightful little granddaughters, now ages three through nine, staying with her. Her grief was turned to joy as she experienced an almost miraculous transformation, returning to her role as a loving mother and grandma. She experienced a personal revival, seemingly getting younger before our eyes. Her vitality, vim, and vigor were inconsistent with her age of seventy-four years. She was in her glory, making blueberry pancakes for breakfast, playing school with the girls in the classroom she had arranged for them in the basement, teaching them old songs that she had learned as a child, and telling them stories of her childhood before tucking them into bed. "Grandma Jean" snuggled each of us in her loving embrace. I again experienced what it was like as a little boy, being coddled and comforted by the healing balm of her maternal spirit. Mom loved every minute of it. So did the children. And so did I.

We spent that precious time doing projects like painting the house, taking her with us to mission presentations that we would give on Sundays at supporting churches, and going to the local theater, where ticket prices were so cheap we didn't even need to sneak in candy. We did a lot to fill that time, and also did a lot of nothing, for just being in the presence of Grandma Jean was enough. Her kindness, coddling, and home cooking provided the healing balm we all needed. Those were six of the most magnificent months I've experienced in my entire life. But in time it just wasn't enough for me.

My sense of self-worth had taken a hit in PNG. I was not only looking to rebound and redeem those three years, but I was also hoping to prove myself. I wanted to believe that the time hadn't been wasted and, therefore, the experience could benefit me personally and propel me forward professionally. In no time, I began receiving offers from congregations in Wisconsin. There were a lot of churches that needed a pastor, and it wasn't every day that they could get one who was seen as somewhat of a celebrity, having served overseas as a missionary. Each of the congregations that contacted me provided a prime opportunity to be close to Mom and my other family members. Deceiving myself into believing I was equipped to serve the Lord in unique ways, I desired something else, something unusual and out of the ordinary. I was looking for a situation I believed to be worthy of my ample arsenal of abilities, extensive experiences, and ecclesiastical expertise.

So instead of staying in Wisconsin, I accepted the "Divine Call" to the Mission Lutheran Church in Las Cruces, New Mexico. It *had* to be the place God wanted me to be, if for no other reason than because of the name itself. It was a mission church, and I was a missionary, or so I fancied myself to be. It was a case of mistaken identity. There was so much more than just the name of the church that enticed me: the intention of the congregation to start a Lutheran elementary school, undertaking outreach to the campus community, and if all went well and we grew in numbers like I expected to, starting another congregation sometime in the future. Here was the opportunity to excel, achieve, and allow me to believe that, indeed, I was a successful servant of God. It presented the very real possibility of redeeming myself, rescuing my pride, and making up for all that I had done wrong. Such thinking, a result of a big ego and a small faith, has many negative effects, not the least of which is creating inauthentic and phony followers of a god of one's own making. My four years of seminary and six in ministry had taught me to excel in the fine craft of hypocrisy, of putting on pious appearances for the purpose of trying to impress others. Rather than doing what I wanted, like staying close to my aged mother in a place I had grown up and loved, I instead made the choice to leave home to chase a spiritual pipe dream cloaked in self-righteousness.

How convenient to co-opt God into becoming either one's crony or scapegoat, and then either crediting the divine for giving us what we think we want or criticizing God for the disasters that we most likely deserve, too often the result of our own making. I was no exception, satiating my shattered self-confidence by once again sacrificing to the false god that is worshipped by those who are driven by success. Thus, in the pursuit of doing something or being someone special, I abandoned the one person in my life who loved me the most. My mother was again left alone to try and make sense of this unpredictable, uncaring, and inconsiderate path her son was on. Though she never said it, Mom didn't want us to leave. She had been in heaven, having her grandchildren in her home, cooking for her family, having someone to love, and who loved her. She was faced with the reality of her advancing age, wondering, I'm sure, who would care for her when she was no longer able to care for herself. For a brief time, she had her answer: her son and his family. Though it wasn't possible for us to live with her indefinitely, we could stay nearby. She could still see us frequently, maybe even come to church with us sometimes. Who knows, maybe if circumstances warranted, she could even eventually live with us. She would have someone to care for, and who would take care of her. Those, I'm convinced, were her thoughts, her hopes, her dreams.

Those dreams were shattered as she watched us load up the truck and leave. I can still see her the day we pulled out of her place, standing alone in front of the garage, waving goodbye. Mom always looked at the bright side of things, looking for rainbows in stormy weather and silver linings behind each cloud. There was one to be found in our relocation to New Mexico, as Mom would spend most of each winter with us. The warm and sunny weather would grant her a much-needed reprieve from the cold Wisconsin snow, which she dubbed "the dirty four-letter word." Nonetheless, it was a poor substitute for what could've been. To her credit, and as a testimony to the type of mother she was, she never asked the question I've been asking myself ever since: "Why didn't you stay?"

I got everything I thought I wanted in New Mexico. The elementary school was started, with a new educational wing being built to house it. Outreach to the university students went well, quickly accumulating a considerable cohort of students. In addition to doing service projects across the border in Juarez, they gathered weekly for dinner and Bible study at our home. Attendance at church services grew so quickly that we had to make plans to expand the size of the sanctuary, and in time to start another congregation. Our family was thriving as well. My wife was studying to be a nurse, the girls had settled into their schools, and we were making friends. The people I was serving were pleased, and that meant the world to me.

As the youngest child and only son in the family, I grew up being a pleaser. I learned at a very early age that being a "good boy" was rewarded. Parents unwittingly and unintentionally provide a picture of God for their children. The idea that if good behavior pleased my parents, the same principle must apply to God took root. It made perfect sense for me to conclude that if my parents were happy with me then God must be as well. Sunday school, confirmation, youth group, and other church functions became an important part of my spiritual life, and I pursued them with the same fervor that I did getting good grades, excelling at sports, and being class president. This mentality of pleasing in the spiritual realm reached a zenith when I mentioned to my folks at the age of thirteen that I had thought of becoming a pastor. Their response was one of elation, and thereafter, it was the only career path that was possible for me. How could I not do that and disappoint them and, by extension, God?

The failures in Chicago and PNG were the first ones I'd experienced in my life, making the success I was experiencing in New Mexico all the more meaningful. I was back in the familiar place of trying to please others, and perhaps God. It seemed as though it was working. God was making His pleasure obvious by recompensing me with what appeared to be almost a Midas-like touch when it came to the projects that were being pursued. I was back in my comfort zone. Though I credited God with the success, deep down I was convinced it was mostly my doing, a result of my own efforts and abilities. I concealed my pride with a thin cloak of false humility.

It's hard work being a modern-day Pharisee, wearing pride and self-righteousness as a badge of honor. But I was perfecting the craft. I knew that God loved everyone, but it seemed that He loved me just a little bit more. After all, didn't I deserve it? I subscribed to a motto similar to the one expressed by the pig on Animal Farm; "All animals are equal, but some are more equal than others." In church terms, it was translated as *"Jesus loves you, but I'm His favorite."* I didn't express it outwardly, careful to give the impression of pious pastoral humility, but deep down, I believed it. After all, I had given my all for God to do the Lord's work.

The sacrifices I had made by going to PNG had not gone unnoticed by the Divine, or so I believed, and now I was being rewarded. The quid pro quo of works righteousness, which I regularly railed against from the pulpit, was firmly set in place in my mind and spirit. I felt as if I was a little more holy, a little more pious, a little more educated, and a lot more dedicated than the common people who sat in the pews on Sundays. I had proven it by going to the inner city of Chicago and then PNG. Now, I was proving my devotion to God by leaving my mother and extended family to accept my calling in New Mexico. I had done everything God asked of me, and more! Everyone was pleased with me, or so I believed.

Trying to please hundreds of people all the time is an impossible task that many clergy nonetheless try to accomplish. I had gotten a taste of it in Chicago, but it came to full fruition in New Mexico. Added to the day-to-day ministry challenges of preparing studies, sermons, teaching and attending meetings were the extra duties like visiting the sick, performing funerals and weddings, managing staff, and providing counsel for people trying to navigate life. More daunting than any of this was trying to meet the never-ending demands and desires of a large contingency of people, each with their own opinion of how church should be. Most members who attend churches don't realize how exhausting it is for pastors to try accommodating the preferences of so many people. And if they did realize it, they might not care. For whatever reason some of the attendees feel it's their prerogative to weigh in on anything from the quality of the sermon to the color of the new carpet in the fellowship hall, to the style of clothes a spouse or daughter is wearing. Attempting to be all things to all people is all-consuming, and eventually exhausting. Added to this is the expectation that the pastor is supposed to be available 24/7. It's not unusual, even on days off, to get a call from a council member wanting to talk about some business matter in the church. What's more, the pastor is expected to respond immediately to any unexpected or unplanned event in the congregation. One simply can't refuse. There are innumerable incidents that come to mind, one of which I will briefly mention simply for the purpose of illustrating the point.

Early in my tenure at the congregation in New Mexico, I received a phone call on Saturday morning. Saturdays were my days to spend with family as the girls weren't in school. On that specific day, I was responsible for watching the kids, while my wife was attending a women's retreat, for church no less. Mid-morning, I received a phone call from one of the church elders, Thomas, who called to inform me that Dorothy had been admitted to the hospital. I had to go visit her, but the girls were too young to leave at home alone. I packed them into our van, drove to the hospital, picked up a small get-well present from the gift store, and deposited the girls in the waiting room.

I looked at my oldest, Katie. "I need you to keep an eye on your sisters while I'm in the hospital room with Ms. Dorothy."

Even though Katie was only ten, she was accustomed to the role of big sister that she was expected to fill. "Okay, Dad. I'll watch them. But how long are you going to be gone?"

"I'll just be a few minutes. Just stay put, and I'll be back soon."

I hurried to Dorothy's room, gave her the gift, had a brief conversation with her, followed by a short Bible verse and prayer, and made my exit to gather up the girls. The entire incident transpired in perhaps fifteen minutes in total. I felt good about being able to juggle my dad duties along with my religious responsibilities—that is, until the following day. After church, Thomas cornered me in the vestibule.

"Why didn't you visit Dorothy in the hospital yesterday?" he asked in an accusatory tone.

"Oh, I visited her yesterday morning. I prayed with her and read some passages from the Bible to her."

Thomas gave me a skeptical look. "I'll check with Dorothy's family to see what she says." The next day, he called me. "Dorothy says you only stopped in for a few minutes. Her family says she was very upset that you didn't stay longer. Next time, do better," he chastised. The previous pastor, who was older and childless, had spent much more time on his hospital visits, and I was expected to do the same.

Expectations. It is impossible to meet them. Trying to do so takes its toll not only on the pastor, but on their spouse and family as well. Pam and the girls were always expected to compromise and give of themselves for the sake of the ministry. They were compelled to fully participate in every congregational activity, from teaching Sunday school and staffing the nursery, to helping with church potlucks and organizing the Christmas pageants. One Saturday early in the Christmas season, my four girls missed a practice for the Sunday school Christmas pageant. That evening, I received a call from the pageant's director. She was outraged that the girls hadn't been there. After going on a verbal tirade, she reminded me of the responsibility that my family had to set an example for the other families in the congregation. Repeated incidents like these, which are the norm rather than the exception in organized religion, wore me and my family down. It is a slow death by a thousand cuts.

By my sixth year of ministry in New Mexico, I was quickly approaching burnout, a malady common to clergy. I didn't recognize it then, and even if I had, I wouldn't have admitted it or asked for help. The constant day-to-day demands of trying to meet the never-ending needs of others were becoming overwhelming. Petty grievances and criticisms were all too common among the godly parishioners, and slowly, I was dying inside. There were daily reminders that I was not being all things to all people, as St. Paul demands. Though Lord knows I tried. The wear and tear on me were not overtly evident to the congregation. I hid it well. Another skill of clergy: hiding feelings and frustrations, and then developing unhealthy habits to deal with them. This is so detrimental and damaging to both heart and soul.

Extra-marital affairs and a variety of addictions, whether to alcohol, drugs, or pornography, are the rule rather than the exception among the clergy. Though I would occasionally binge drink at social events, my addiction of choice was exercising. Training for marathons took up much of my free time. I would rise early to do my daily workout. Most Saturday mornings started with a fifteen- or twenty-mile run. It was an acceptable coping mechanism and a way of escape. When I returned home, the energy that should've been expended on my family had been depleted. Too often, they were the ones who were sacrificed on the altar of my sacred service, and like the scapegoat in the Old Testament, they were on the receiving end of my disappointment and disillusionment. While nurturing others, I failed to adequately nurture them or myself. While building up others, my family was being torn down. While giving the congregation my time and the best I had to offer, my family had to settle for leftovers. After six years, the unreasonable expectations and ongoing demands of a growing church were wearing me out. I badly needed a break! I needed to get away, not just for a vacation, but for something longer. I had heard about sabbaticals, so I began to investigate the possibility of taking a study leave.

Once I had settled on the idea, I was like a convict hatching an escape plan. I began to obsess over how I would make my break from what I had begun to perceive as the prison of pastoral ministry. There were several obstacles, the first being to get my wife and daughters on board. Pam had graduated from nursing school and had been working nights for about a year. Though she was adventurous and had eagerly jumped at the chance to go to PNG and move to Las Cruces, I wasn't at all convinced she would be willing to interrupt her newly launched career and uproot the family to accompany me on this escapade. It would be a huge sacrifice for her to put her career as a nurse on hold and venture into the unfamiliar territory of medicine as practiced in another country. I failed to fully consider the fact that by this time she had begun feeling the full effects of my disillusionment in parish ministry and the toll it was taking on me. My sleepless nights and short fuse were far-too-common occurrences. After talking about it, she agreed to consider the possibility and would do some research on the requirements for working in another country as an expatriate. She also encouraged me to find a graduate program that I could apply to which might provide a future alternative to the ministry. We both did our due diligence, and the result was that she discovered the process of getting clearance to work overseas, and I landed on pursuing a master's degree in church history at Glasgow University in Scotland.

Why Scotland? I don't know. It just came to me. Maybe it was a dream or epiphany. Or maybe it was my infatuation with the romanticism of the place. Ancient castles like Edinburgh and Stirling, historical figures such as William Wallace and Rob Roy, and renowned saints like Columba and Aidan. It might have had something to do with my ancestry, which could be traced to the Lamont clan. Or maybe it was just God. Maybe I was listening to my intuition and spiritual imagination and following an inner calling of the Spirit, something frowned upon in my conservative Lutheran faith tradition. Maybe unwittingly, God was orchestrating events in my life that were beyond my ability to comprehend or control.

But what about the children? Yes, they were adaptable; after all, we had dragged them to numerous different places already in their short lives. But they would have to leave their home and their friends for a year, a seeming eternity in their young lives. We called a family meeting to get their input and answer their questions. Selling the idea to them by appealing to their vivid imaginations and painting a picture of a place with quaint stone cottages and towering castles that housed princesses like Rapunzel from fairy tale lore helped to convince them that this would be their own opportunity to step into their own fairy tale. After answering a few questions, like whether they'd have their own bedrooms or if they'd get to go to dances, they each voiced their approval.

The next hurdle was getting permission from the congregation. Would they go along with a year-long break? Would they provide at least a partial salary? Would I have a job when I returned, or would they have decided to move on from me? Though unheard of in my church organization, study sabbaticals were becoming more common in other church traditions. Meeting with the board of elders first, I provided biblical precedence for the concept. Basing decisions by proof-texting Bible verses was very important to the literalistic-leaning Lutheran church body to which I belonged.

I gave them examples of the seventh-year sabbath rest commanded in the Old Testament, as well as to the occasions where Jesus Himself had to take a break from the demands of his ministry. To my delight and surprise, they approved, and after pitching the idea to the congregation, it was decided that I would be granted my request! During this time, I would receive a quarter of my salary. In addition, they agreed to pay for my school tuition, a very generous gesture on their part. The next nine months were spent putting necessary pieces in place to leave, such as finding a renter for our house, a pastor to care for the congregation in my absence and making connections with the members of St. Columba's Lutheran Church located in East Kilbride, a suburb of Glasgow. By the grace of God and no little human effort, the pieces all fell into place, and in August of 2001, we set forth on our family adventure and my quest to find respite and a renewed desire to do ministry.

Our itinerary had us landing at Heathrow in London and then renting two cars to make the rest of the trip north to Livingston, Scotland, where we would meet Dan and Elaine, members of St. Columba's. After navigating the airport and making it to the rental car company, we divided into two groups, with my wife driving one car with two girls, and me driving the other. We had carefully mapped out our route but had failed to account for the high volume of London traffic and the very real possibility of getting separated, which is exactly what happened! As we approached the initial major roundabout, the first of many new experiences when driving in Scotland, I took the wrong exit, and my wife, driving the car behind, was not able to follow. We didn't have cell phones—this was 2001, remember—and so for the remainder of the drive, approximately seven hours, we made the trip separately.

Kayleen and Molley, my second oldest and youngest daughters, were with me. Like me, they were free spirits. So when it was determined that we wouldn't be able to find the others, we decided to make the best of an unfortunate situation and start our stay in Scotland with an adventure. Our journey included stopping to buy strawberries along the road and taking a detour to the famed castle city of Durham. We finally arrived at our destination hours late, only to be greeted by a combination of relief and irritation by Pam and the other two girls.

Dan and Elaine, who would turn out to be an absolute delight, hosted our family. Though we had never met them, they welcomed us with warmth and affection. It would be our first taste of Scottish hospitality. Dan was "Canadian by birth, Scottish by choice," as he liked to say. Short and slightly rotund, he resembled a modern-day pirate, with a beard and earring to boot. He was very jovial, always ready with a clever anecdote or humorous joke. Elaine fit the bill of a "Wee Scottish Lass" perfectly, standing just shy of five feet tall with blazing red hair. Dan lovingly called her "The Queen of Scotland." Their love story began while on holiday in the Dominican Republic. Dan was in a life transition, recovering from a divorce and having sold his business, looking to start a new life. Elaine was on holiday, vacationing with a group of friends. Elaine wanted to learn how to play poker, and one of the dealers directed her to Dan, who had quickly developed a reputation as a high roller. He eagerly agreed to show her the basics. The next day, he looked for her at the resort and, upon finding her, asked her to dinner. They still have a photo of that first date on display on their coffee table. It went so well that six months later, Dan moved to Scotland and opened the only mobile hot dog cart in the country—or so he claimed. For £3.50, one could buy an all-beef hot dog and a soda that could satisfy one's hunger, and fill the heart as you listened to a joke or an encouraging word from Dan.

We piled into Dan and Elaine's two-bedroom, one-bathroom townhouse. At night, the small living room and dining room were transformed into bedrooms for the four girls. In the morning, we would stay in our rooms until Dan and Elaine left for work, and then have free rein of the house. They were more than gracious in making room for us. It was our first introduction to the kindness of the Scots, but it wouldn't be our last, as we were grateful recipients that year of the gift of hospitality that was so common in that culture.

After three weeks, we had acquired a small three-bedroom apartment in Chapelhall, a small village approximately twenty minutes east of Glasgow by train. Referred to as a "Scottish Special," a euphemism for a very basic and inexpensive place, the apartment was just big enough for the six of us, comprising three small bedrooms, a tiny kitchen, dining room, living room, and one bathroom. Moving from a four-bedroom ranch-style home with a large backyard and two bathrooms into the cozy confines of this modern-day version of a Scottish cottage was initially a challenge, but in time it provided an opportunity for a type of togetherness that we hadn't experienced back home.

Initially, the girls, ages sixteen, fourteen, twelve, and ten, faced the most difficulties in adjusting to their new environment. Added to the normal challenges of adolescence, a tough time under the best of situations, they were each the new "American kids" at their respective schools, where they were treated by some as celebrities, and by others with scorn. "Kids will be kids," my mother used to say, and the ability to be both kind and cruel is no respecter of cultural boundaries. The girls experienced both during their year. There were academic as well as social challenges. The school-work was much more rigorous than what they had left in their previous schools. The three oldest attended the Protestant junior and senior high, while the youngest, Molley, attended the Catholic elementary school just up the street. Dividing the girls between Protestant and Catholic schools was unheard of at the time, that part of Scotland still being vehemently partisan and parochial when it came to religion. This division even played out on the pitch, the term used for a soccer field, where loyalties were divided between Rangers, the Protestant soccer team, and Celtic, the Catholic one. Later, we discovered that the ecumenicity which we took for granted was an anomaly for many of the people among whom we lived. The year provided the girls not only with the opportunity to experience another culture, but also to grow much closer as sisters, solidifying the bond that had been forged in the fire of PNG and would be strengthened beyond breaking during the difficult days to come.

In the mornings, the three oldest girls would board the bus to their school, while their mom would catch one to her workplace. Pam had been hired to work in an asthma and allergy clinic, which provided a much-needed boost to our meager income. Three days a week, I would catch the train to Glasgow, exiting at Charing Cross to take the charming walk through Kelvingrove Park, adorned with flower gardens and small peaceful ponds. Glasgow University, historically the second oldest in Scotland, stood majestically on Gilmore Hill, the site where it was moved in 1870. Its Victorian architecture, with a medieval-like appearance, included ramparts and cloisters.

The Scotland I experienced was much different from that which my other family members did. When not attending my few classes I would either wander the peaceful grounds surrounding the university or sequester myself on one of the upper floors of the more modern library. Pam and the girls were living a much more real and raw life. There was a vast difference between the demands they encountered in their daily routines and the delights I experienced in mine. The dissimilarity began to fray at the edges of our marriage. By the end of the year the dissonance had moved to the center of our marriage. The tension increased, and arguments became more frequent, usually over petty matters like whether to take a walk, who would do the shopping, or what kind of excursion to make on the weekend.

Those weekends were eagerly anticipated as they provided a release valve for the family's frustrations. We would explore iconic historical sites like St. Andrews, the Glasgow Cathedral, Edinburgh Castle, and Holyrood Palace. We also managed longer getaways, one to Inverness and Loch Ness, and another for two weeks to Amsterdam, Brussels, and Paris. By the end of the year, we had crammed in as many adventures as we possibly could before running out of time and money. I had floated the idea of remaining in Scotland to pursue a PhD at Durham University, but Pam and the girls would hear none of it. They were more than ready to go home. As our year ended there remained one place to visit: Iona.

I had learned about this island, the cradle of Christianity in Scotland, in my studies that year. There was an Abbey there, as well as an ecumenical community that dedicated itself to life in community and maintaining the cause of the gospel for the marginalized throughout the world. As luck, or divine design, would have it, I came across an old, framed painting of the Abbey in a thrift store, which I purchased for two pounds. It was an invitation, a reminder, perhaps even a beacon extending an invitation to this historical place, renowned for being a destination for spiritual pilgrimages. In time it would assume a prominent place in my home and serve as a reminder of that magical year in Scotland, and a constant reminder of my desire to return. Iona became the holy grail upon which I set my heart that year. Finally, in June, mere weeks before our departure, we trundled off in our small car to take one last trip to the destination that would mark the culmination of our adventure and kindle within me the fire of the Spirit to one day return.

Though we had made many trips during our year, this one was especially meaningful due not only to the destination, but because none of us knew if or when we would be back. Soon, we were traversing the Trossachs, a regal region wherein lies the more familiar Loch Lomond. This scenic area provided the setting for numerous novels, such as *Rob Roy* by Sir Walter Scott. In modern times it also was the setting for the Disney Pixar movie *Brave*. The ascending heights and long-fingered lakes reflected royal hues and azure blue more than sufficient in and of themselves to satiate the senses. But they serve merely as an appetizer for the sensual feast that was to follow. We began the ascent into the historic Highlands, home of those ancient Scottish legends like Robert the Bruce and Mary Queen of Scots who live on in modern-day lore. Looking down at the Lochs (lakes) and gazing up at the Bens (mountains), one could easily envision in the mind's eye William Wallace standing with a horde of hardy Scotsmen, ready to do battle with the English in defense of the freedom of this magical land. The landscape whispered an invitation to sit back and drink deeply from the beauty in which one was engulfed. Even the girls, cramped together in our small car, didn't complain, so taken were they with the natural beauty!

After a few hours of navigating the narrow roads and natty roundabouts, we arrived at the sleepy seaside village of Oban, home of a very nice whiskey, where we would take the thirty-minute ferry ride on the Caledonian MacBrayne ferry to the small village of Craignure on the Isle of Mull. We were all transfixed as we stood by the boat railing watching the sleepy seaside town recede into the distance. The brisk spring wind whipped across the bow, at times refreshing us with the sudden spray of seawater. En route, the distant ramparts of Duart castle, the ancient home of the Maclean clan, and the site of the movie *Entrapment* starring Sean Connery and Catherine Zeta-Jones, met our gaze. Disembarking at Craignure, we began the last leg of the journey, a thirty-seven-mile drive on a one-lane road across the rocky and sometimes relatively barren landscape of the Isle of Mull. As we drove farther along this small highway toward what felt like the end of the world, it was difficult to believe that our destination was once considered such a central part of the history of Scotland, serving as a destination for kings and commoners alike. Finally, we arrived at the small seaside village of Fionnphort, where our family, weary from the all-day trip, stomachs slightly queasy from the roller-coaster-like car ride, quickly settled into our bed and breakfast. Across the sound, the Isle of Iona was clearly visible, the picturesque seaside village with Scottish-style houses dotting the shore, and further in the distance, the grandeur of the Iona Abbey, majestically rising up out of the surrounding green fields.

The following day, we arose early to eat a hearty Scottish breakfast of eggs, scones, mushrooms, tomatoes, ham, sausage, beans, and of course, black pudding. Outside, brightly colored skiffs gently bobbed by the quay, where we eagerly made our way to take our first outing of the day. We boarded one of the boats to take us to Staffa Island. The small vessel bounced gaily over the waves, with the cold spray from the North Sea kissing our cheeks. After roughly forty-five minutes, we saw Staffa rising from the ocean. We disembarked and trod the somewhat treacherous path along the slippery stones at the foot of the cliffs into Fingal's Cave. Renowned for its natural acoustics, it was easy to see why Mendelssohn was inspired to compose *The Hebrides* overture after visiting this place. As we moved slightly beyond the opening and deeper into the cave's depths, Katie and Pam, both gifted with beautiful singing voices, spontaneously joined together for a duet of "Amazing Grace." The sound of that sacred song in that setting surpassed any I'd heard performed in a cathedral crafted by man.

Exiting the cave and walking to the top of the island, we were greeted by puffins, small black and orange birds, darting up and down the sides of the island, and diving from the sky to the turquoise sea. The vista was breathtaking on this clear and sunny day, allowing us to see in all directions. We sat down together to fully imbibe this naturally inebriating experience.

We would have remained there for hours, but our time was limited, and our sights were set on our destination: Iona.

As we passed back through the sound on our skiff, the Abbey commanded our attention. From a distance, it lacked the majesty and grandeur of some of the other cathedrals we'd visited during the year. Yet there was something unique about the Iona Abbey. It was as if the magnificent building was a muse, calling out to us across the sea, inviting us to come closer to be enchanted by the Spirit living there. We eagerly answered that call. Arriving at the dock, we exited the boat and boarded the nearby ferry to take the short ride that would deposit us at our destination.

Suddenly I found myself standing again before the green door that had entranced me. Traipsing through time to relive the past events that had brought me to this moment had ended. Only a few minutes had passed, enough to allow the others to walk up the path ahead of me, but it was as if time had been suspended and I had been away for years. Still relishing the reverie of the journey I had just taken, I quickly hurried to catch up with the rest of the family who were now far ahead.

Before us loomed the Abbey, dwarfing the two Celtic crosses that stood out in front. Paying our admission fee, we passed the hill where Columba prayed, the well whose waters were said to provide countless pilgrims with the miracle of healing, and the small chapel that served as his shrine. As we entered through the large wooden doors, we stood at the top of the stairs of the sacred structure. We had visited numerous sacred sites during the year, whether in Scotland or Europe, but this one was different for me. Here I felt immersed in the Spirit, bathed by the ineffable Presence of God, who was not only transcendent but immanent. Despite the cold, I felt warm within the Iona Abbey, not only surrounded, but seemingly embraced by the spirits of those who had lived and died here. I was overcome, perhaps even possessed, by a Spirit different from any I had ever encountered before. This Spirit was not a theological concept, biblical idea, or church teaching, but a Living Presence that permeated this place. This Spirit was deeply personal, yet profoundly universal, intimately connecting and uniting me to God and to all that ever was or would be. I was keenly aware that God was in this isolated isle in a way that was distinctly divine! It was unlike anything I'd experienced that year, or for that matter ever before in my faith life. Taken by surprise, I sat down to soak in this experience of wonder and awe.

The family tarried there for a time, taking in the stone surroundings and the relics on display from the past. Too soon, they were ready to move on. We slowly walked back along the path upon which we had come, taking our time to stop at the small shops along the way. The return trip was uneventful. I was, for the most part oblivious to what we were seeing, as I was preoccupied in my thoughts with what I had just experienced. I contemplated the overwhelming sense of being fully immersed in the very essence of God which permeated that place. This island felt like coming home. It seemed as if it was where I belonged. I sensed an aspect of God I had never experienced before. I had been in the ministry for fourteen years, but I couldn't recall ever feeling a deep connection of God that drilled into the depths of my very being that I felt there.

In the days to come I realized that a huge part of my spiritual life up to that point had been missing. The previous year of study had satisfied my quest for the theoretical and theological knowledge of God but was a poor substitute for being in the mystical Presence of God. Something spiritually significant had shifted during that short time at Iona, and not only did I ponder the profundity of that place, but I also began to question: *How had my faith and love for God been so shallow? How had I reduced the spiritual life to filling pews and pleasing people?* That gave way to other more central questions, *Who was I, really? What was I doing? Who was I doing it for? What was I believing? Who was I believing in …if anyone?* Those questions would lead me to question my own calling into ministry, and what mattered most to me. I replayed the epiphany I had at Iona throughout the short time we had remaining in Scotland and long after my return to the U.S.

We spent the last few days packing up our belongings, having a farewell party catered by Dan, the hot dog man, and wishing our friends farewell as we prepared for the journey back to the U.S. The family was eager to get home and be reunited with their friends whom they'd left almost a year earlier. I was dreading it. Not only had I relished the reprieve from my religious duties and the freedom in living a more authentic life apart from being a pastor, but I also felt like I was leaving home to return to a foreign country. Like a prisoner who has violated parole and is being returned to his cell, I was returning to what I saw as my incarceration. My mood blackened. I had no clue how dark the ensuing days would become.

The next few years would introduce me to what is best described as the dark night of my soul. I would journey with my mother into the bottomless pit of Alzheimer's, my extended family becoming estranged because of it; I would experience pastoral failures greater than any I'd ever known; and my marriage of twenty-five years would end in divorce. Perhaps I could sense the changes that were going to take place, even then. Maybe God was sending me a signal at Iona, trying to equip me for what was to come. Maybe those last days in Scotland served as some type of holy harbinger, foretelling the future. I don't know. What I do know is that I hadn't left Iona alone. Unbeknownst to me at the time, the Spirit of the Living God who had met me at Iona was going with me, and would one day lead me back again.

Part Two

LEAVING MINISTRY

FOUR

Descent

GOD LEADS INTO THE DARK NIGHT
THOSE WHOM HE DESIRES TO PURIFY.
—St. John of the Cross, *The Dark Night of The Soul*

"You know, I'm considering divorcing you." Those words, delivered while we were celebrating our twenty-fifth wedding anniversary at the Dreams Resort in Tulum, Mexico, were a verbal whiplash.

The darkness that had been gradually descending on my life became impending doom. I felt as if I were experiencing a complete emotional eclipse. The threat of divorce had been brought up by Pam at other times in our marriage in the heat of an argument, but never with such serious intent. This time, I knew that it was more than a response designed to defend a position in an argument. The hidden meaning behind her words was, "Get ready. The hammer is about to fall." Though we had experienced what might be considered the normal marital stress and strife common in marriage, there was nothing irreparable. Or so I deceived myself into believing.

Granted, the previous few years had been somewhat rocky. We had moved to Colorado five years earlier to live in a place and serve a congregation that I thought would be perfect. The two years in New Mexico after my sabbatical had been difficult. Many congregants felt betrayed or abandoned, and a few subtly resented me for having left them for such a long time. Resistance to my pastoral leadership had increased. On one occasion a full-blown argument broke out in a church council meeting between me and one of my detractors. The magic of the Midas touch which I had possessed before leaving had evaporated.

A year after my return, Mom was diagnosed with dementia. My world was turning. I felt out of place. And I missed home—Scotland. The signs were clear: it was time to leave. I contacted my ecclesiastical supervisor to distribute my name to other congregations as a candidate for a "Divine Call." That's what the church organization called it. But by this time, I had become a cynic, unsure of what exactly made it divine. The methods described in scripture for choosing priests, pastors, or apostles were noticeably missing. On the part of the congregation, it mirrored what went on in any secular business, and on the pastor's side it was essentially a job interview. What made "the Call" most divine was where it was located and how much it paid. Divine downward mobility was a rarity among most clergy I knew. Climbing the ecclesiastical corporate ladder was the norm. I was no exception. I took the initiative and put into motion the process necessary to find a congregation in a different place, preferably Wisconsin, so I could be close to Mom and help in navigating this new landscape of Alzheimer's.

It didn't take long for an opportunity to come, though it was to Colorado rather than Wisconsin. It seemed like the perfect place to live; geographical beauty of the Rocky Mountains, better schools and universities for my wife and daughters, a church that appeared to be the perfect fit—and, of course, paid more. But all that glittered was not gold, and the journey we had taken north from New Mexico quickly went south. There was considerable conflict in the congregation, difficulties my daughters had adjusting to their new schools, the untimely death of my wife Pam's nephew, and, of course, the challenges of Mom's progressing dementia. Nothing seemed to go right, whether personally or pastorally.

After four years in Colorado, I realized that Pam and I were having marital difficulties. I attributed them to the stress from my ongoing conflicts in the congregation, the pressure my wife was under to finish her nurse practitioner degree, and especially my mom's Alzheimer's disease which had driven a wedge between my siblings and me. My relationship with my four sisters, with whom I'd been quite close throughout my life, had fractured. Decisions for Mom's well-being were being made unilaterally by the two sisters who held the Powers of Attorney, to the exclusion of the other three of us. My sisters canceled a minor surgery that would've vastly improved Mom's quality of life and placed her in a nursing home without my knowledge or assent. It was maddening. I would make occasional trips to impart my opinions and stir the pot of strife and discord.

My lingering regrets and guilt for not having made the move to be near Mom ate away at me. The pressure release valve was my anger. I was angry at my sisters, other family members, doctors, ombudsmen, nursing home administrators, and even God. Why had He allowed this to happen to my loving mother? I became perturbed, prickly, and a habitually unpleasant person to be around. By the time the dementia finally stole what little was left of Mom, I was as broken emotionally as she was physically and cognitively. My wife received much of the collateral damage from my pent-up anger and resentment. Ministry, Mom, and family demands of daughters leaving for college left little time for us. It was a toxic environment that we were trying to navigate. I realized too late that all of it would have lasting consequences on my marriage, my family, my ministry, and me. It would launch me onto a journey in life that I could never have dreamed of making.

All hope was not lost, however. Though our trip to Mexico revealed the seriousness of the sinking ship we seemed to be on, perhaps another trip, this one to Scotland, could help us reverse course. Pam agreed, albeit a bit reluctantly and with the caveat that we take Molley and her best friend, Haley, along. Not coincidentally the trip would coincide with our actual wedding date, July 14. The time in Scotland almost ten years previously had provided a wonderful year of respite from the pressure of ministry. Maybe it would have the same type of healing effect on our marriage. Scotland was calling, and I hoped that our return, especially to Iona, would result in redemption.

Shortly after our arrival, I realized that the hopes that I had entertained for the trip were going to evaporate like the early morning mist on the Scottish moors. The distance that had been growing between the two of us became greater as we began our trip. Conversation on the seven-hour plane ride was kept at a minimum. Pam did her best to keep space between us and limit physical contact. She pulled away from my attempt to hold hands. A kiss was out of the question. Intimacy, which I so desired, was a mere figment of my imagination. The sleeping quarters at Dan and Elaine's house, our first stop, were incredibly uncomfortable due to the small bed we were forced to share. Our conversations were courteous but strained and superficial. The distance between the two of us only grew worse as the days passed. What had begun with so much hope twenty-five years earlier now seemed hopeless.

We had planned to spend July 14 by ourselves in Glasgow. Shortly after boarding the train for the trip in, my wife held her left hand before me, displaying the ring I had placed on her finger on our wedding day. "See," she said, "I'm wearing it for you." The intended message behind the gesture was clear: this was a kindness being extended reluctantly for my sake, not hers. It was a piece of jewelry that may have had monetary value, but very little when it came to our marriage. It was being worn temporarily on this memorable day, but it would soon be removed permanently.

When our train pulled into Queen Street Station, we quickly exited the train, as if trying to escape being too closely tethered, and began our venture into the city. We were surrounded by a bustling crowd yet shrouded in silence. What I had meant to be a celebration of our time together turned into a death march. We spent the day mechanically going through the motions, taking in familiar sites more like tourists than husband and wife. It was more a test of endurance than a time to enjoy one another's company. Tony's, which had been one of our favorite places to dine, served more as a time of toleration than celebration. Following our lunch, we agreed to cut the day short and trekked back to the train station. We sat next to each other, each preoccupied in our own thoughts. What I had hoped would be the start of a new beginning in our life together instead marked the beginning of our end. What I had hoped would be an occasion for commemoration, and the beginning of our restoration instead became yet another step on the path of further deterioration. It took the truth of that train trip to make me see the vast distance and irreconcilable difference that existed between us.

There remained one last hope: Iona! Only a miracle could save the marriage, and Iona was the one place that could provide it. Pilgrims had made the journey there for centuries, seeking some form of salvation. There was the Well of Eternal Youth and Pool of Healing, which locals believed had restorative powers. Why, legend had it that Columba had even saved a man from the Loch Ness monster. Certainly, his spirit, if not the one I had experienced there ten years prior, could rescue us from sinking further into the abyss of the deep waters of marital dissolution.

The four of us stayed at a bed and breakfast for two nights at Fionnphort, the small village across the sound from whence one catches the ferry to the island. As we disembarked on the isle of Iona, we perused the small shops and then walked the path to the Abbey. As we entered through the massive wooden doors, I peered down the long aisle and was reminded of watching my beautiful bride walk down the aisle of her home church so many years prior. As the reality of our present discord settled in, I longed for a renewal of vows and a chance to make right all that was wrong. As a pastor, I had seen many others trying to negotiate with God. Now, I was the one desperately attempting to bribe and bargain my way into God's good graces. *God, if you will only see me through this trial, I promise I will be better, sacrifice more, give you whatever you want. I will be the man you expect me to be, the husband she wants and needs me to be.* I pleaded with God to make right all that was wrong, not only in my marriage but with me, some of which I was aware of, most of which I wasn't. I was dying for divine intervention. I didn't want my marriage to end. I asked God to use the Spirit of Iona to heal my marriage.

After purchasing a few souvenirs in the gift shop, we began the stroll back down the narrow lane. On the way, Molley suggested that we pose for an "anniversary kiss." I think she knew (how could she not?) that something was terribly wrong. Suddenly, there it was: the small cottage with the green door. It was the portal that had transported me on that journey through my past on our last trip. Perhaps it had the power to propel us into a healthy marriage on this one. We paused in front of that picturesque little place and posed for a brief, dispassionate peck. How different from the kiss exchanged all those years earlier when we pledged our undying love in front of the altar of a church surrounded by the warm love of friends and family. That kiss in front of the green door was as chilly as the day, as distant as the place. There, in front of the small green door, we exchanged our last kiss.

It's human nature to try and rewrite our own stories, to do our best to alter the course of events which seem inevitable in the forlorn hope of changing the ending. The ending I was hoping to write was the kind found in fairy tales; kissing and making up, growing old together, and living "happily ever after." That may be the stuff of storybooks, but it is not how real life works. That ending was my fantasy, but the trip to Scotland shocked me into reality.

We returned home only to resume the rapid journey on the road to marital perdition. She left home in October and filed divorce papers in November. We appeared in court three days before Christmas, a holiday to remember. Mediation took place in February, and the divorce was final at the end of March. Twenty-five years over and done in a matter of mere months. I was devasted spiritually as well as emotionally. The solid rock of religious beliefs upon which I thought I had been standing crumbled beneath me. The faithful God I had been taught to believe in had forsaken me.

Our four daughters, in their late teens and early twenties, suffered severely from the divorce. Each of them handled the termination of our marriage in different ways. The youngest, Molley, a senior in high school, spent many nights with me crying buckets of tears in the safety of what was once our family home. The oldest, Katie, a newlywed, found herself disoriented as her parents' marriage was ending just as hers began. Kayleen and Meghan, both attending the same university, found some sense of solace in having one another to cling to as the earth gave way beneath them. The divorce affected each in their own unique ways, some of which even they may never be aware of.

I wish I could say I was strong for my daughters, but I wasn't. They were hurting, and the personal darkness I was experiencing prevented me from providing the empathy and compassion necessary to help them cope with their pain. I had all I could do to alleviate my own hurts, let alone help to assuage theirs. Having Molley still at home provided some consolation and gave me a reason to get out of bed in the morning. Some days I had her school activities and sporting events to attend. Most nights, I had someone to eat dinner with and talk to. This time with her was precious, but would provide only a temporary reprieve, as the clock was ticking until her graduation.

The proverbial silver lining amid the dark post-divorce clouds was my relationship with all four girls. It had been good before, but the divorce made our father-daughter bonds even better. The time we spent and conversations we had together were priceless. Oftentimes, I had nothing to say, nothing that could be said, so I would just listen. And at times I would talk. I was raw and vulnerable. Perhaps at times, maybe too much so. But it was an honest expression of love. And it made a difference. We stumbled together through the dark valley of divorce, refined by the fire of our family's meltdown, and as a result formed an unbreakable bond that remains to this day.

The dark days passed slowly, but the year went quickly. Far too soon graduation day arrived for Molley. It was a time to celebrate her accomplishments, and at the same time dread her pending departure. The summer flew by far too fast, filled with activities and necessary preparations. In early August, the day I had done my best to ignore finally arrived; my last daughter was leaving home. She had chosen to accept a volleyball scholarship at a small college in Missouri, an eleven-hour car ride away. I had always relished our summer road trips, but this one felt to me like throwing down the gauntlet. I had arranged to spend a few days with her there to help her get oriented and settled in, and to try and avoid the inevitable for as long as possible. Finally, the morning came for me to say my goodbyes and give her one last hug and kiss. Watching her wave as she slowly receded from view reminded me of the day I watched Mom do the same as she stood in her driveway. I held the tears in until I was out of sight. And then I broke down. I cried for the first hour, and then intermittently for the next ten hours after. Today, many years afterward, I can jokingly say that I don't know what was more difficult, saying goodbye to my wife or my last daughter when she left home. But at the time it was no laughing matter.

As I walked back into my house, the reality of my new life met me. I was confronted with life-sucking silence and solitude, and the recognition that I was now alone. Completely alone. I had no one. All that I loved most in life, my mother, daughters, and wife, were gone. The huge dwelling which had once been a home had now simply become a house. Like me, it was a lifeless shell and a constantly cruel reminder of what had once been. That space that was once filled with life and love now seemed very vacuous; the laughter that had rattled the walls was replaced by a cavernous quiet. It was as if I had entered a museum that had closed for the day. I sat alone in the darkness for hours, replaying the course of events that had led me down this dark alley, this dead end. The emotional descent into the arena of regrets was inevitable. Asking the unanswerable questions while questioning my own role in it all; feeling forsaken and as though God had forsaken me; lacking faith in a loving God and not caring. I was desperately trying to feel something, anything divine. Finally, I surrendered, not to God, but to fatigue and the futility of it all.

I awoke early the next morning. What day was it? I didn't care. Not Sunday. That was a relief. But I still had to play the part of a pastor, which promised to keep me busy, distracted, and financially secure. If nothing else, my sense of duty and "calling" gave me a reason to get out of bed in the morning. Waiting to greet me were two visitors with whom I had become quite familiar: guilt and shame. They had occasionally stopped by before, but now they announced their intention to take up permanent residence with me. Now that everyone was gone, I could no longer ignore them. They began badgering me with questions, like:

"How can a holy man be divorced?"

"What does this say about your love for your wife?"

"What kind of a man abandons his mother? Are you going to abandon ministry as well?"

"Your family left. What's the purpose of living like this?"

And perhaps most damning of all: "Who do you think you are? Pretending to be a good man and pastor. You're a failure. Why don't you stop pretending and just give up?"

These were only a few of the questions that assailed me. I lacked the strength to resist them, and so I listened and gave credence to the condemnation. The pointlessness of my new status began to assault me like a pack of jackals, the attacks intensifying in the days, months, and years to come.

I made myself get out of bed, practically stumbling down the stairs to sit with my coffee, my Bible, and my swirling thoughts, doing my best to hear a different voice; the voice of Another. As I sat in my emotional and spiritual stupor, the painting of Iona that I had brought with me from Scotland and that hung in my small study caught my attention. I focused more carefully on it, recalling not only the time spent there, but trying to recapture a modicum of the peace and serenity I had felt. Slowly the significance of the simple picture began to morph from merely being a repository for memories to a beacon for future possibilities. Iona was the place where I felt the deepest connection to God and myself. The God who seemed so distant now had been so very close at Iona. For a few minutes I allowed myself the luxury of imagining what it might be like to go back to Iona. For the briefest of moments, I thought I sensed that Spirit I had met there present with me. I was enamored. And then it was gone. Nonetheless, those moments made an indelible impression that I carried with me that day, and in the days to come.

Most days I wore a clerical collar to work, common attire for pastors in my tradition. I felt somewhat self-conscious as I inserted the white tab, seeing it as the finishing touch to a costume I was wearing. I was dressed up as a respectable clergyman. It was a one-man act in which I played the part of a person of great faith. I had assumed this role many times before, giving the impression that I was a bit "holier than thou." I did my best to provide an answer for all matters pertaining to God. But now the script was rapidly being rewritten. I was still a clergyman, but in this new performance, I was portraying the pious person who believed that there was joy in suffering, a divine purpose for everything, and that God would work "all things out for the good of those who love him and are called according to his purpose."[1] It was a well-rehearsed script that I had practiced and perfected. It felt like I was mindlessly and carelessly uttering worn-out clichés with the mistaken assumption that saying such things somehow made a difference for others. They certainly didn't to me anymore. For that matter, I'm not sure they ever had. Behind the scenes, when the curtain came down, and I was offstage,

---

1 A reference to a passage found in Romans 8:28. I came to despise these types of biblical proof-texts which serve as common and worn out cliches for far too many Christians.

there was a shell of a man who was hurting horribly and hurtling toward the abyss of a new kind of dark and unholy trinity: Depression, Doubt, and Desperation.

In retrospect, the theological premises that I had been taught and parroted for so long didn't provide an antidote for the sickness infecting my soul. I found no comfort or consolation in the doctrines and dogmas I had learned. All of it seemed so erudite and irrelevant. It was hollow, pointless, meaningless; soul-sucking rather than life-giving. Nor did I find solace from others I turned to for support in my hour of need. With few exceptions, other clergy were distant, especially uncaring, and crass in their interactions. Perhaps I expected too much from mere human beings who could provide too little. One thing became clear: the very people who were theoretically most capable of providing counsel and comfort were either the most unconcerned or uncomfortable doing so. Very few initiated contact. Even those I considered friends seemed clueless about or intentionally detached themselves from what I was experiencing, as if divorce might be contagious. It seemed to me that they thought I had been stricken with a contagious disease that they were afraid of catching. I felt like a modern-day Hester Prynne, wearing a large letter *D* for "divorced." I watched as the "priests and Levites" passed by me on the other side. Years later, I had the opportunity to ask one pastor, whom I had considered my friend, why he hadn't contacted me, if for no other reason than out of curiosity. His response was sobering and slightly shocking: "Because I didn't know what to say!"

Painful though it was at the time, this distancing of other pastors was a gift in disguise because it brought me closer to the real source of comfort. As the reality set in that co-workers, congregational members, and counselors would be of little help, another realization took its place: God had not abandoned me. In retrospect I realize that on this downward descent into my own personal hell, God was closer to me than I realized at the time. In my past, I had focused on knowing *about* God. Now in my hour of darkness, I began to find solace in being known *by* God. It was this descent into a place of desperation that I became an unwitting participant in the spiritual experience of being drawn to the God whose presence was most imminent, and who one could experience in just such a place. This God was meeting me not in official teachings of church but in a far more personal way, bypassing my well categorized and compartmentalized belief system so as to be present in a very intimate way. I began to get to know a God who had previously been a stranger to me, whom I had never really experienced in my innermost being. I was being drawn into a love greater than all those I had lost. It created in me a novel desire not to preach or teach, do something for or give something to God, but to simply nurture this new experience of being close to God. It was a descent into something truly Divine.

For years, I had begun each day by bounding out of bed and sprinting into my exercise routine. Long-distance running had been an addiction of sorts, my preferred means of greeting the morning. But exercising when running on empty emotionally is an almost impossible task, and so my routine changed. Each morning began slowly, spending time trying to find a reason to get out of bed. Inevitably, there was always at least one I could come up with: someone who was sick or in the hospital who needed a visit, a meeting or counseling session, or at the very least savoring a cup of coffee. Descending the stairs from my bedroom, I would sit in the silence of the early morning darkness, by myself but not alone. Hands clasped as though in prayer around the warm cup, I longed for God to again reveal the gentle Spirit. Sometimes, I sensed The Presence, other times I didn't. As darkness slowly turned to dawn, I would open my Bible to a small segment of the scriptures. After a time I would write down something meaningful on a small slip of paper, and later, I would place this small sacred treasure in my pocket, retrieving it at various times throughout my day when the clouds began to descend again, or a jolt of encouragement was needed. It was as if the Spirit would softly speak into my soul, breathing some life back into me. That became my daily routine. And as it began to take hold, this Spirit began to take hold of me. Previously I had seen God as distant, harsh, demanding, needing to be appeased. This God with whom I was becoming more familiar was so different. If there were any expectations, it was simply to be in that calming and peaceful Presence, to spend time doing nothing but sitting in the sacred peace, calm, and serenity I so longed for.

In time, I began to anticipate this gentle whisper, this still small voice, which eventually led me into the awareness that I desired and needed something more. I longed for this deliberate and dedicated time with God. This desire was not of my own doing, but Spirit prompted. It led me to being planning an intense multi-day personal retreat. I had never taken such a retreat due to my busyness, the suspicion of anything that seemed too Catholic or that it was too touchy-feely. Or maybe I was just afraid of what I might discover if I had that much time for self-examination, exploration, and introspection. I recalled a friend telling me about the Abbey of St. Walberga, a community of Benedictine nuns, located in a secluded valley not far from the Wyoming border. It seemed the perfect place to be, so I set my heart on a mini-pilgrimage.

FIVE

Divine Loneliness

Immediately upon arrival, I was bathed in peaceful silence and soothing solitude, surrendering to the serenity of the sacred surroundings of
nature as well as the sanctuary. Though I was by myself, I was surrounded
by God in this natural setting, as well as by the nuns, living icons of what it
means to live a life devoted to God. My housing was in a dormitory some
distance from the church and priory. I was given a small, simple dorm room
with a single bed. There was a common area, a kitchen, and a small library
just down the hall. Though tempting, on the first day I avoided the library
as my purpose was to focus on prayer, not on reading, as had been my
habit. But on the second day, the urge to see the selections of spiritual
literature available was unavoidable. As I perused the various selections,
my eager eyes happened to alight on one with the intriguing title, *"Invitation to Love."*[1] I am convinced that the hand of God had placed it there.
That pearl of great price would propel me further along this new path
upon which I had been placed, a path of spiritual discovery and personal
transformation.

---

1 Thomas Keating, *Invitation to Love: The Way of Christian Contemplation* (London, Bloomsbury Publishing, 2011).

Love. That is what I had lost, and what I was looking for. The love of a mother, the love of a spouse, the love of two sisters, the love of a church, the love of God, and ultimately the love of myself. This book provided not only an invitation to the God who *is* love, but also a new way of not only believing, but receiving God's love. Like so many other attributes of God, I had previously considered God's love to be a theological matter to expound upon rather than an intimate personal gift to experience. Like a drink to be savored, I read slowly, pausing frequently to ruminate on the love of God that was being not merely described, but brought to life in a way that I had not known, or quite possibly had long since forgotten. I began to appreciate what, or whom, had been meeting me in my dark mourning.

The first chapter on emotional happiness introduced spiritual concepts I had never encountered before, such as the journey into the spiritual life with God being a descent, the occupational hazard of Pharisaism for religious people, and how one unwittingly functions out of the false self.[2] The prescription for the healing of a broken heart and a shattered life is not written in theological treatises that parse the finest points of systematic theology, nor is it a matter of doing more intense study so as to have a more precise, accurate, and right definition of God which can be used to defend one's understanding against other religious opponents. Rather it is a reclining upon the breast of Jesus as John the Beloved Disciple did at the Last Supper in order to rest safely and securely in His loving heart. This book not only diagnosed my spiritual condition but delivered both a salve for my hurting soul and a signpost that directed me on this new way, which, though previously untrodden by me, had been well traversed by many others. In time, I would be introduced to fellow travelers, both ancient, like Theresa, Julian, and Eckhardt, and modern, with names like Nouwen, Brown-Taylor, Merton, and Manning. I came to a personal epiphany in that library, which I pondered for my remaining days of the retreat and carried back to the enclave of my house. There, in the early morning darkness, I began to not only gain an appreciation for, but also an affinity with others who had experienced their own dark nights of the

---

2 Keating, 6.

soul and found light as they settled into the tranquility and peace of the love of God.

The time on retreat passed by far too quickly. I dreaded leaving. However, I left no longer dreading each new day, but almost looking forward to it, greeting the darkness I was experiencing and the daylight gradually dispelling it. Though I was by myself, I knew I wasn't alone, being in the company not only of God but of my spiritual companions sent to accompany me along this new path.

One might expect that with this new awareness, the darkness of my soul would give way completely to light. But that was not the case. If anything, my spiritual dissonance became even more evident as my inner self began to gently rebel against my external vocation. The pastoral role was becoming more and more foreign and daunting to my restless soul. My life split into a duality of sorts. In one sense, I began to feel and see something besides futility; my heart of stone began to beat with a love that fueled something that seemed to be an almost embryonic faith. As this nascent spiritual experience began to grow, there was a simultaneous dissonance I became aware of. My pastoral identity, which I had spent so many years polishing, became more and more of a stranger to me. It was becoming difficult to recognize that person. An increased dissonance and growing divide between the authentic self that I was becoming more aware of, and the role of pastor which seemed to be that of a play-actor, became more pronounced. My spirit became a little more desperate as I peered into the deep divide between the new person I was meant to be and the old one that I still pretended to be. My pastoral duties became more burdensome than ever, as my sole desire was to pursue this new identity in God.

Contrary to what some might believe, the spiritual life is not a constant ascent onto mountaintops of transfiguration where one experiences perpetual joy in the Presence of God—at least not in this life. Rather, it is a series of setbacks that test and refine one's soul. I was still heartsick over my lost earthly loves and attempted to numb the pain experienced in my recent past by desperately seeking new love.

I began to venture forth into the world of dating with fear and trepidation. It was an unfamiliar landscape I hadn't traveled for almost thirty years. My motivation was selfish, self-serving, and unhealthy. All my life, there had been a woman, whether a mother, sister, wife, or daughter, who provided comfort to me. Now, I had no one. A counselor had told me that a person should remain single for one year for each five years of marriage. That translated into five years of singleness for me. Unfathomable! I began desperately looking for love. But I had little to give and only wanted to receive. It was a disaster!

I would be in a relationship for a very short time, like a parasite getting all I could out of the newfound host, and then I would be overcome with guilt and shame and break it off. How could I, a man of God, who had taken vows to be faithful to one woman unto death, live as though they meant nothing, as though a piece of paper had invalidated them? Legally I was divorced, but in my heart, I wasn't. I felt like I was cheating on a promise, and the shame of being unfaithful to that sacred marital bond ate away at me. I had been devoted to Pam to the extreme, even averting my eyes from the occasional cleavage so clearly on display at the communion rail, and now it felt like I was committing adultery. In my desperation, I did my best to show up for the kind yet unfortunate women who crossed my path and provided me with temporary comfort, but it was a sham. As we were parting ways, one of them blatantly told me, "You're still in love with your wife." She was right.

I also sought to assuage my pain and loneliness in other ways, mainly through alcohol. Growing up in Wisconsin, I was introduced to beer at a young age. Being a typical teenager, weekends with my friends often-times included getting some beer and drinking at someone's house whose parents were away, or possibly in our cars on a deserted road or hard-to-find farmer's field. That bad habit was shelved during my marriage. Though I would occasionally drink in social settings with friends or parishioners, we seldom kept any alcohol in the house. That all changed when I found myself alone.

Four evenings a week were usually spent at church or on church-related tasks. On free nights, it became a habit for me to meet up with a friend at a bar. There was one who became my drinking buddy. In time, that became the default button for my social activities. It wasn't unusual for me to leave work, go to a bar, spend three or four hours drinking, and then drive home intoxicated. My growing dependance on alcohol as a coping mechanism and subconscious attempt to deal with my depression became more serious.

Without a family there were no more shared meals, school events to attend, or anyone to discuss my day with. Alcohol was my attempt to fill the void. The solitary evenings began to press in on and oppress me. Fridays were my regular day off, so Thursday nights were the beginning of my weekends. One stands out in particular.

I had returned home after an especially trying week, though each week was beginning to feel that way. Emotionally drained after another rough week at church, trying to meet the demands and needs of others while neglecting my own left me anxious to start my weekend. It was a relief to have another week behind me and two days to try and gather myself for Sunday. Rather than zoning out in front of the TV, which was also my habit, I poured myself a glass of red wine and sat down at my computer to surf the internet. Perhaps unwittingly delving further into denial, so common in the world of alcohol dependency, I navigated to an article on the coronary benefits of red wine. It was all the incentive I needed to pour myself a glass from the half-full bottle of merlot. My father had died of an aortic aneurysm at the age of sixty-two, so this seemed to provide some justification for my drinking. Quickly draining that one, I poured myself another. *If the first was good, the second must be better*, I told myself. Soon, that bottle was empty. I opened another. I adeptly drained that one to the dregs as well. By the end of a very short evening, I was fully inebriated. What concerned me the next morning was not the splitting hangover headache, but the grinding guilt at having gone down this pathetic path alone. Guilt, which I had perfected with the help of church teachings, is the feeling that one has done something wrong. But for me, it went beyond this. I felt great shame. Not only did I have a problem, but I also felt that there was something seriously wrong in the fabric of my very being. It was as if all my past transgressions were piling on, and I was being buried not only under unresolved guilt but the added burden of suffocating shame.

I had judged myself and believed God was judging me, based on the inventory of sacrifices I made and what I believed were the resulting rewards. I had waded into the gang-infested waters of the inner city. I had taken my family halfway across the world and exposed them to unimaginable risks in the process. I had started a school and grown a church, something I took great pride in. In each instance, I made a significant sacrifice for Christ and the church. I paid the price to advance God's kingdom. As a result, I believed God had blessed me with a happy family, a stable home, and a successful ministry—until now. Now, I found myself questioning all that I did, why I did it, and who I did it for. I was questioning the faith that had failed me and the fickle God who was the object of it. I was nothing but a divorced pastor, alone in an empty house with empty booze bottles comprising part of the decor. What did God think of me now? I was in foreign territory, trying to navigate a desert landscape where I was hopelessly lost...and thirsty.

The intervening two days until Sunday were spent on a roller coaster of self-justification and self-flagellation, on the one hand trying to vindicate myself for the sins that I'd committed and on the other condemning myself for the poor excuse of a person I had become. I was tapped out physically, emotionally, mentally, and especially spiritually. Two days later, as I prepared to again go through the motions of a Sunday morning as I had done so many times before, I was still overwhelmed by the unresolved emotions broiling beneath my calm, clergy surface, and the self-loathing that had taken up residence in my soul.

A traditional Lutheran service begins with a general confession of sins. Historically, confession had been practiced individually with a priest, abbot, abbess, or a fellow brother or sister in the faith. That changed in Protestant churches after the Reformation. It was seen as being too Catholic. And yet there was still the perceived need to cleanse oneself before entering the holy space of a sanctuary and the Presence of God. In the Lutheran church, it was called "The Common Confession," in which the congregation would join in admitting in a general way not only to sins committed, but also to sin as an inherent condition. The general confession was very impersonal and benign, providing a sense of holy anonymity, which allowed one to feel like a secure sinner in its non-specificity. One could acknowledge being "by nature sinful and unclean," all the while admitting to anything, everything, or nothing at all. We joined our voices with that of David in Psalm 51 to repeat the spiritually damaging idea that we were all conceived in iniquity, born sinful and unclean, and deserved eternal death and damnation. That was followed by the reminder that this condition of original sin had caused us to act out against God and others in our thoughts, our words, and our deeds. After the confession was corporately verbalized by the congregation, there was a time of silence provided just in case people wanted or needed to reflect on their own particular sins. In the spirit of the self-righteous Pharisee, I had at times silently prayed in my heart, *God, I thank you that I am not like other people.*[3]

I was racked with regret and remorse and overcome by the conviction that I needed to get real, not only with God and myself, but with others as well. My most recent dive into drunkenness had been done alone. There was no one else to blame for that. During the time of silence, I thought about my sins and the mess that my life had become; I contemplated my role in the divorce, the seething anger directed at my sisters during the death of my mother, the occasional temporary trysts, and, of course, the alcoholism. Perhaps for the first time in a very long time, I was finally honest with myself and God. It felt good. Very good. So good that in the time it took to go from the start of the service to the sermon, roughly fifteen minutes, I was led on a bold new course of action: I discarded my sermon manuscript, so carefully crafted as was my custom, and upon which I had poured hours of preparation, and instead went off script and spontaneously came up with one on the spot. The spirit (whether mine or God's, I have no clue) had moved me to speak from the heart. I began with these words: "Every Sunday, we stand here and confess our sins. I don't know what you confess, and it's none of my business. I don't even know if you take it seriously or not. The truth is that most Sundays, I don't. But today, I did. I want to tell you what I told God today in my confession. This past Thursday night I went home and proceeded to get drunk. Really drunk. All by myself. It wasn't the first time I had drunk too much. In fact, I've been doing it a lot these past few years, but always with others. This time I did it all by myself. Like a common drunk. That's what I confessed to God this morning."

---

3 The full account is recorded in Luke 18:9–14.

I wanted to share more. I wanted to tell them about the other pits I had been plunged into and was trying desperately to climb out of. I longed to unload all the guilt and shame that I carried, that I was a divorced husband who had ignored the warning signs from my ex-wife until it was too late, that I was a selfish, prodigal son who had failed his mother in her hour of need, that I was a pastor who half the time didn't believe what he was telling others to believe, that I was a man guilty of sins that are common to his humanity. I wanted to tell the congregation how the guilt of all of it caused me to inwardly loathe myself and outwardly cloak myself with false piety as a means of self-protection for fear of rejection and losing my profession. But I couldn't. Not because of pride or my desire to make a good impression but because "godly" people aren't prepared to hear that kind of raw truth being propelled at them from the pulpit. They weren't ready to hear that their pastor was struggling just to make it day to day, trying to cope by turning to things other than God and the gospel and all the glib remedies that good Christians are supposed to turn to and depend upon in our hour of need. They didn't want to hear that their pastor was just like them—certainly no better and sometimes worse. They weren't ready to catch the pastor when he fell off his pedestal. In this case, the truth would not set them free. But it did that very thing for me! Just that little bit of honesty provided a taste of what it would be like if I could be genuine, authentic, and just myself, without the worries of what other people expected me to be.

That was a groundbreaking Sunday, providing a powerful spiritual transition. It was the Sunday I realized I no longer could do what I was doing, cloaking myself in clergy robes and performing the deceptive divine dance that went with it. That was the Sunday when I clearly saw that while God might be pleased with a sincere and genuine confession (though I've come to question this as well), most people in that congregation certainly weren't. They preferred the road more commonly traveled, paved with pretense and false piety. They preferred their pastor to be something other than genuinely human, and to play the part that had been assigned to him. That was the Sunday I stepped down from the pedestal I had so proudly been standing on, and out from the pulpit I had been hiding behind. It was the Sunday that I began to renounce the role of being a pastor and embrace my real identity as a beloved child of God. It was the Sunday I took my first steps out of the pulpit and pivoted towards the new path that I was being placed upon. It was the Sunday that I started to genuinely believe that God sees us as being so much better than the worst thing we've ever done. It was the Sunday that I no longer cared what people thought of me.

That was the Sunday of my epiphany, the Sunday that the lights went on, the Sunday that God whispered to me in the dark cave of my confession to cut the crap and get real. I was not a horrible human being, no matter how I felt or what I did. There was something better and far beyond being a sick and suffering sinner. That may have been part of my condition and the cause of some of my suffering, but it was not my identity. Nor was my identity found in being a pastor, which I would learn was merely a pretense that prevented me from being genuine and authentic. It was a career I no longer cared about, a job I no longer enjoyed, a vocation that was bringing me closer to damnation than salvation.

Following that service, many of my parishioners were probably left wondering, "What in the hell just happened?" For me, it was a huge step out of my own personal hell. The heavens had opened. I was filled with deep peace. I had taken the first step toward resurrection, and though I didn't know where that path led, I finally felt that I was stepping out of the darkness and into the light.

SIX

Divine Departure

LIKE SOMEONE WHO HAS BEEN LOST FOR YEARS
IN A FORGOTTEN PLACE, YOU REJOICE IN BEING FOUND.
WHEN YOU ARE DISCOVERED, YOU THEN DISCOVER YOURSELF.
—John O'Donahue, *Walking in Wonder*

Rupert Sheldrake, an English scientist, was asked what he would rec-ommend as the most significant change for the new millennium. His answer: "Every tourist should become a pilgrim." On my previous two trips to Iona, I had been a tourist. On my third trip, I would become a pilgrim.

This pilgrimage to Iona represented both a beginning and an end; the end of my old life and the beginning of my new. It began to fall into place as the pieces of my old life fell further apart. My ministry, hanging in the balance after my divorce, began to inch closer and closer to the edge. I was approaching the end of my badly frayed rope. I was hanging on by a thread. I keenly sensed that soon I would lose my grip. I had experienced ministry and life storms before, but this was an unrelenting hurricane. In the past, I had found refuge in my family and some close friends who provided a solid foundation during the squalls. Without this bedrock, I didn't have the strength or faith to face the tempest alone. I couldn't find the eye of the hurricane, no matter how hard I tried.

The process of returning to Iona a third time was accelerated by a small coalition of unhappy congregants. In the weeks following my public confes-sion from the pulpit, they began to mount a more intentional opposition movement. Some of them deliberately avoided me after Sunday services. A few others made passive aggressive comments at church council meetings. What had been gossip whispered in private became very public criticisms. There were countless reasons that might have motivated these members to want to get rid of me. Perhaps it was because from early on in my ministry, I had rocked the boat by desiring to improve the acoustics in the sanctuary by removing the carpet and the orange 1960s-like pew cushions. Perhaps it was some of the new ideas I had introduced, like using some of our extra land to house a community center or participate in a program run by the local Catholic Charities to provide temporary housing for the homeless. Both of these were met with vehement opposition by a very vocal few and died on the vine. I'm certain that others simply didn't like having a divorced pastor. Maybe it was just a struggle for power and control and had little to do with me directly. Whatever it was, the antagonism of the opposition was ramping up. I'd experienced internal strife at previous churches, but nothing like this. It felt like a mutiny, or like a small lynch mob that was coming after me.

No matter what I did or how hard I tried, I couldn't please them. In retrospect, I shouldn't have made such an effort to do so. Trying to please people is an impossible trap into which many pastors fall, resulting too often in their downfall. The rugged individualism and "Made in America" mindset have thoroughly saturated most churches. There are as many agendas and personal opinions as there are people populating the pews. Priorities are placed not on healing the sick or giving sight to the blind, but rather on keeping the building looking nice, coming up with programs to attract newcomers, and of course generating more income.

But there was something else going on, which I believed was spiritual warfare being fought on the battleground called grace. I had begun to fully grasp the meaning and value of grace, especially for sinners in whose company I now firmly planted myself. I stopped putting so much emphasis on sin, stopped emphasizing the common sins that gave congregants such satisfaction condemning and focused more on the ones that seemed more pertinent to those regularly populating the pews on Sundays, like smug self-righteousness, and instead focused more on what manifestly mattered to God and was so clearly portrayed in the words and life of Christ: love, mercy, and forgiveness. Rather than preaching condemnation for sinners, I proclaimed God's comfort poured out upon all of us. This included those whom "good Christians" were most uncomfortable with: the addicts and alcoholics, the adulterers, and those living alternative lifestyles, judged to be unacceptable. I did my best to make the congregation see that homosexuality is no more damning than the addictive sins that good Christians conveniently overlook in their own lives, whether those be pride or pornography, greed or gossip, or the insatiable desire for wealth, power, and control. The message of grace falls hard on the ears of the self-righteous, and those clinging to traditional beliefs and customs are convinced that some people really are more deserving of God's love and mercy. The elevation of grace and public defense of the downtrodden hardened the hearts of those powers arrayed against me.

The gossip mill that had been churning eventually made its way back to me, and I heard what was being discussed behind my back. In essence, I was unworthy of my calling and a poor reflection on the congregation. It is hard to admit, but looking back, they were right, at least partially: I was unworthy. But not for the reasons they believed. If sin disqualified someone from ministry, Jesus' ministry would've been a solo act without any disciples. The personal pitfalls so common in pastoral ministry put clergy in good company with heroes of the faith, whether Moses or Mary Magdalene, Peter, or Paul. The biblical record is clear; sin doesn't disqualify someone from ministry but makes them more qualified for it.

The opposition reached its apex at a congregational meeting held a month before Christmas and two months before I would finalize my decision to leave. In my Lutheran tradition, church councils and voter assemblies have ultimate authority and are the way God intends for church organizations to do business. There is no little irony in this considering the historical account of Jesus, who was condemned by a church council and whose crucifixion was demanded by a voter's assembly. Not surprisingly, my end as a pastor also came at one of those meetings.

I knew there was trouble brewing, though I had not anticipated the extent of the vitriol that would be leveled against me. Ironically, it took place almost exactly ten years after my first meeting in that same congregation. I remembered the arguments first encountered over the biblical role of women in the church. The church organization forbade them from being pastors. But could they be elders? Could they serve as the council president? Could they be active in ministry in other ways without violating the supposed sacrosanct scriptural principle of a woman not exercising authority over a man, a principle which many tenaciously clung to? It was distressing, and I knew then that I had stepped into a hornet's nest. What I didn't realize is that, in time, I would be the one stung.

Now I had become the cause of their consternation. As the congregational meeting, which took place after church services on a Sunday, wore on, I sat in silence. Though the tone was similar to that one that had taken place ten years earlier, I was at peace. God spoke clearly through the arguments, some defending me and my job while others criticized me. They didn't remove me as their pastor, but the die had been cast, and I came away with perfect clarity: *I'm finished here.*

The cacophony of the criticisms in that last congregational meeting continued to ring in my ears as I returned home later that afternoon. I welcomed the silence as I walked through the door, allowing me to contemplate all that had just occurred. As I settled into my chair, my eyes affixed once again upon the painting of the Iona Abbey. Now, God was speaking a different message through this simple piece of art, which had become my own living icon. I longed to return to the place that had once filled me up spiritually. Whether moved by impulsiveness or God's Spirit, I went to the Iona Community website. To my delight, I discovered a program for volunteers. One could go to the Abbey and live and work there for free. I began to fill out the application. It was extensive, and there was no guarantee that I would be accepted, as they received numerous applications for a limited number of positions each year. Nonetheless, I completed the online form. The process felt cathartic, healing, and somehow holy, as if guided by the Spirit of Iona. However, it was soon forgotten as the busyness and demands of the Christmas season were upon me.

Christmas takes on a different meaning when one is responsible for putting it on. The exuberance, enthusiasm, and unbridled joy of the season

I had experienced for so many years with my family and ministry had disappeared, replaced by a sense of dread. There was no joy in decorating the Christmas tree, singing heart-warming hymns, putting up decorations, or making, baking, and eating Christmas cookies. It had all become mere drudgery. I had always loved Christmas, but it was different that year. I felt, well, Grinchy, struggling to see the light amid the darkness.

Despite the difficulties, a sign was given to me during the Christmas Eve service, this one also having to do with a baby boy. My oldest daughter, Katie, was there with my year-old grandson. He had a meltdown shortly into the service and had to be taken out of the sanctuary. I interpreted it to mean that I should leave also. Iona came to mind. That was the gift I was hoping for, waiting for, praying for.

The new year arrived without news from Iona. It had been well over a month, and I was becoming concerned, especially after a conversation with my friend Rob, who I had asked to write my reference letter. He was planning a trip to the U.K. that year, and so naturally, the conversation turned to the topic of my application. I mentioned how much I enjoyed my previous time spent in Scotland, and how badly I hoped to go back to Iona. "Oh, I'm sorry, I completely forgot to write your letter," Rob announced. My dream of escaping from ministry and going on pilgrimage had ended before it would ever begin. I have since become aware that it is then, when hope is no longer visible on the horizon, and all seems darkest, that daylight is about to dawn. On January 19, I received that email notifying me of my acceptance.

Some people might consider my actions impulsive or irresponsible. In retrospect, there were other possibilities that perhaps I could've pursued. A six-month sabbatical would've relieved some of the pressure and provided much-needed respite. But I was in a dark and desperate place; all that mattered was getting a glimpse of light. The only way to do this, I was convinced, was to take permanent flight. If it was foolish, it was Spirit-inspired foolishness. If it was a crisis, it was God-ordained rather than a mid-life one. It was not a temporary reprieve I needed, but a transformation into a new life that could only be gained by putting to death my old life and being resurrected anew. It was not a vacation, but a transformation that I needed.

Throughout my years of ministry, death had become an all-too-familiar friend as well as an unwelcome adversary. Though the goal of life is spending eternity in the Presence of God, a reality that can be experienced in the present, the process of getting there is painful. And the actual occasion of the spirit leaving one's body, drawing a last earthly breath, is anything but beautiful. I had been with many as they made the transition from life to death. I had observed and experienced it professionally and pastorally with many parishioners. It was this process that I felt I was experiencing personally.

I was dying of loneliness. Although I was surrounded daily by people, my personal pride and position as pastor prevented me from being close to any of them. I was dying from trying to make things right in my life when I knew everything seemed so wrong. I was dying from playing the part of a "good pastor," pretending to be someone I wasn't. I was dying from trying to meet the expectations that I believed God and others had for me. I was dying to be myself, warts and wounds, scars and scabs, and have others accept me as such. I felt like I was on life support and desperately needed resuscitation.

So did the congregation. Throughout my years in ministry, I had witnessed more than a few pastors who overstayed their welcome, resulting in the stagnation and disintegration of clergy and congregation alike. Though not many members had left, it was certain the mass migration would soon begin; the sparse attendance during the Christmas season was proof of that. It was apparent that the congregation was in the doldrums, merely trying to stay afloat. I found it imperative for me to shove off so that they could set sail again. The email I received from Iona on that dark January day was a gift for all of us.

As I prepared to set forth on my pilgrimage to Iona, I decided to sell my house. On the one hand, I felt as if I had no choice. I was quitting a well-paying job and had no way to pay my mortgage. On the other hand, I was reluctant to do so, as I had poured so much of myself into it. No matter how many schemes I came up with for how to keep it, I would need money to live on as I didn't have any prospects for another job and had no intention to serve as a pastor again. So, the difficult decision to part ways with a place filled with memories, both good and bad, was made. I received an offer on March 17, St. Patrick's Day, and though it was far below what I had hoped to make, I decided to sell anyway. I needed to cut ties with everything tethering me to my past life. I was ready for my new life to begin.

The congregation had planned a farewell for my final Sunday. The most difficult part of my departure was the goodbyes. My father used to say that one should never say "Goodbye" but rather "See you later," as the former was too final. But I realized that this farewell was, in fact, permanent, for I was leaving not only people and a profession, but an important part of what had defined me through so much of my previous life. My false identity as a pastor, to which I had clung so tenaciously, was being buried.

When I walked through the doors of that church for the last time, it was not a "See you later" that I would utter, but a final "Goodbye." Goodbye to the members and friends. Goodbye to twenty-seven years of ministry, which demanded the best I could give. Goodbye to the Lutheran church in which I had been baptized, confirmed, ordained, married, and had buried both of my parents. Goodbye to colleagues, some of whom were friends. And most importantly goodbye to the pastor person I no longer recognized. I was saying goodbye to that person who had become a stranger.

Some of the most sincere and surprising goodbyes came from the most unsuspecting people. A woman, for example, told me that she had very few friends but considered me one of her closest. I was shocked. Only a few years earlier, I was on the receiving end of her vitriolic and public tirade for, in her opinion, failing miserably in my pastoral duties to her dying mother.

There was also a small group of close friends with whom I prayed, partied, laughed, and cried. They were safe, loving, and forgiving. They embodied the best qualities of the Christian faith. It was hard to leave them. Most of them didn't attend the farewell, perhaps because they harbored resentment towards others in the congregation, or maybe they were just grieving. Nonetheless, they served as a lifeline during some of my most difficult days. Sadly, those friendships would slowly fray and eventually fade away. I can still see their faces and hold each of them tenderly in my heart.

And then there were the many, many members of the congregation for whom I had provided pastoral care, but never allowed myself to get close to. I'd been given the privilege of being with so many people during their time of need, and at the time, I perceived the relationship as a one-way street, with me doing the giving. It is clear how clouded my perspective was at the time. Many of the people in the congregation had poured themselves out for me as well, not only with their prayers, but in small yet meaningful acts of kindness expressed as I left in their gifts and kind words.

My eldest daughter, Katie, was the only one of my children that attended the farewell luncheon. It had to have been harder on her than it was on me, for she had been my little "church mouse." As a child, she accompanied me on visits to shut-ins, taught Sunday school, sang in the choir, and while she was in college, she got up early to have coffee with me before the early church service. The church had been her life. I had been not only her dad but the only pastor she had ever known. Now, that portion of her life was ending. She conducted herself that day with grace and dignity and extreme compassion and understanding for her father. At the end of that monumental day, I went to stay at her house, where I would make the final preparations and pack for my three months in Scotland. A few days later, she would drop me off at the airport, where we would again embrace and shed the tears that had become so familiar.

My mother had a favorite saying: "When you're young, you have dreams. When you're old, you have memories." Mom was partially right. I am convinced that dreaming doesn't need to end as we age. We must have dreams throughout our lives. Dreams allow us to keep moving forward with purpose. Dreams give us a reason to get out of bed in the morning. Dreams enable us to cope with the disappointments that life dishes out. When I moved to Colorado, I dreamed of a ranch with cattle. I wanted a place to grow up with my kids and grow old with my grandkids. I had dreamed with my wife of paying off the mortgage early and retiring, getting a VW Vanagon, and taking trips across the U.S., stopping whenever and wherever we wanted, living like vagabonds, a couple of born-too-late hippies. So many dreams... some of which had never materialized, others that had been transformed into nightmares. I was saying goodbye to them all. I could only hope that my departure would give birth to new dreams.

I was dreaming of what Iona held in store for me, dreaming of the people I would meet and the new life that would ensue. I was dreaming that the Spirit, whom I believed was leading me, would help me to clearly see what God was seeking for me. As I finally settled into my seat and the plane began to taxi, I quickly fell asleep, overcome with emotional exhaustion and eager to start dreaming.

Part Three
LOVING GOD

SEVEN

A Loving Welcome

WE HAVE COME FROM MANY PLACES FOR A LITTLE WHILE;
WE HAVE COME WITH ALL OUR DIFFERENCES SEEKING COMMON GROUND;
WE HAVE COME ON JOURNEYS OF OUR OWN WHERE JOURNEYS MEET.
—"The Welcoming Service" in the *Iona Abbey Worship Book*

*T*his must be similar to what St. Columba felt when he first stepped onto the island, I thought as I set foot off the ferry onto Iona for the third time. Stories differ as to why Columba left his native Ireland in 563. Some say he murdered a man, some that he was banished by the king, some that he set forth of his own volition, but they all agree that he sailed with his small group of monks in their coracle until he could no longer see his homeland. It was a pilgrimage for him, though far more arduous and permanent than the one I was on. Yet I felt a sense of connection, camaraderie, and companionship with Columba. In some sense, I felt that our journeys were similar. We were both motivated by the need to escape conflict and find peace, both with a diligent desire to find a more sacred place, both requiring a reset of life and a complete starting over, and both of us were desperate to leave behind the familiar landscape of our lives and leap into the unknown abyss of whatever was awaiting. The difference, and it was drastic, was that Columba would never return to the land that he left. I would.

Though the ferry was quite full, only five of us had come to work as volunteers. Waiting on the jetty for our small group was Kelli, the staff coordinator; Seamus, the maintenance supervisor; and Simon, a young staff member who would become more of a son than my supervisor during the ten weeks. This humble human embodiment of the holy trinity gave us a warm welcome, the first of many that would be extended to every visitor, guest, and volunteer. The staff loaded our luggage into a green van. Almost everyone who came to Iona, I would discover, carried more baggage than met the eye; we each came bearing the emotional weight of life's invisible burdens. Many spiritual pilgrims who washed up on Iona's shores came with unfulfilled dreams, abandoned aspirations, and disappointed desires. Some felt like me, that both life and God had failed them. In time, most would discover that not only did we not need to hide the junk that we brought with us, but that there were many kindred spirits willing to help unload, unpack, and even help carry it for us.

After brief introductions, we began the walk through the quaint village along the one-lane road. It is the only one on the island and runs for approximately three miles. While everyone talked as we walked this simple path, I slowly sauntered by myself, silently reveling in the old familiarities: the fresh sea air, the neatly manicured gardens, the quaint cottages, the occasional cry of a seagull.

Walking up the slight incline from the village, our small cohort passed by the ruins of the nunnery, a small museum, a coffee shop, and a Church of Scotland building tucked behind a small green field. Rounding a corner, we made our way up a small knoll, where I was greeted by an all too memorable sight: the small building with the green door.

I stopped and stood still, the memories of my twenty-fifth wedding anniversary washing back over me. It was only the first of many times that I would pass this door during the ensuing ten weeks at Iona. Each time, I would briefly pause to allow a little more of the power that those painful memories held over me to fade a little further into the distance.

Soon, we came to St. Oran's Chapel and the ancient cemetery that surrounds it. St. Oran was a cousin of Columba. The old stone building that bears his name is the oldest one left on the island, dating from the twelfth century. The story goes that when Oran died, Columba saw angels and devils fighting over his soul. Considering the content of that legend, it is appropriate that the graveyard surrounds the chapel. Many past kings of

Norway and Scotland, including MacBeth, are buried here. Most recently, a modern monarch of sorts was laid to rest in this place, John Smith, former Labor Party leader who preceded Tony Blair as Prime Minister of the U.K. Here, the sepulchers serve as sacred markers, sanctuaries of sorts where one can easily sense the presence of the living spirits among the dead.

Dwarfing both St. Oran's and the cemetery is the Abbey, which shelters both under the shadow of her religious ramparts. Old stones that had been part of the previous Abbey were used to rebuild the present one in the 1930s by skilled, unemployed artisans from Glasgow under the supervision of Rev. George MacLeod. It is a structure that simultaneously conveys the strength and security of the centuries-old faith and the solid rock of Christ upon which it is built, together with the warm welcome that enfolds everyone who enters through its waiting arms. Two Celtic crosses rising roughly twenty feet high stand guard like sentinels in front of the Abbey. St. Martin's and St. John's Crosses are replicas of the originals and serve as reminders of the Celtic Christians who gathered at the foot of many such markers scattered throughout the countryside, beckoning the faithful to worship outdoors in the natural cathedrals of God's creation.

Bypassing the Abbey to the left, we moved through a small stone passageway and into the cloisters, which formed a quadrangle around an open lawn space. A walkway led us through a door in the opposite corner and up an old stone stairwell. Turning to our left at the top of the stairs, we entered the dining hall, or refectory, as it is more commonly called. Six long wooden tables, each capable of seating twelve people, ran the length of it. They reminded me of the long benches in the Great Hall at Hogwarts.

"Welcome to the Abbey dining room," Kelli said. "You'll be spending a lot of time here with our guests. Every day, there will be a mid-morning tea break. Ana has prepared something special for you, scones, which we consider to be the best on the island, to give you a taste of what is to come." With that, we were treated to what truly was one of the most delicious of all Scottish delicacies. Served with butter and raspberry jam, they were truly delectable! This would be the first opportunity to take part in these Scottish delights, but not the last, for there would be daily breaks, deemed a cultural necessity not only for rest and refreshment but for connecting socially with others. Our small group of pilgrims, weary from our day-long journey, sat savoring these sweet treats as Kelli gave us a basic run-down of life at Iona and introduced us to our roles during the time spent there.

Some volunteers at Iona were assigned to work primarily in the kitchen, others in housekeeping, and still others wherever needed as "general assistants." We then received our living assignments, either in Cul Shuna, a small cottage-like dwelling close to the village, or the MacLeod Center. I was assigned the latter, a more modern dormitory-style dwelling that sits at the top of a small hill behind the bookstore and gift shop. With duties and domiciles distributed and the delicious tea and scones consumed, we were invited to make our way to our residences. On our way, we passed sheep contentedly grazing along the path, as if conspiring to bring the 23rd Psalm to life.

Large wooden double doors marked the entrance to the MacLeod Center. To the left of the entrance was the dining hall, where staff, volunteers, and guests congregated twice daily for commonly shared meals. An ascent up a small flight of stairs led to the second floor of the guest quarters as well as the more private living quarters for the volunteers, with two large common bedrooms for women to share and one for men. During my stay, four of us would be sharing the small bunk-house-style accommodation equipped to sleep six. Just outside our room was a small kitchen where we could make breakfast, prepare a snack, or cook an occasional meal. Every space was intended to be shared, including the bathroom and the common area, both located adjacent to the kitchen. The accommodations could be considered cramped or cozy, depending on one's perspective and previous experiences. Some of the more introverted types found this lack of personal space difficult to navigate, but I welcomed the respite from my former life in isolation. Downsizing from over three thousand square feet in my home to about thirty wasn't nearly as difficult as I imagined.

After the brief tour of our new living space, Kelli took her leave, allowing us to get settled. I chose a bottom bunk, and after unpacking my few belongings, tacked my most prized keepsake to the end of my bed: a calendar with pictures of my grandson. While I was sure I would face some challenges during my time at Iona, the most daunting would be the separation from my family and that little guy.

At 6:00 p.m., the evening meal was served. The cooking staff was committed to practicing sound economic and ecological principles, so they primarily served a vegetarian menu. The Iona Community prioritized care and concern for all of creation, not only preaching it but practicing it as well. The chefs continue a modern-day practice that dates to the ancient Celtic reverence for the earth and the gifts she bestows on all creation. Before partaking, one of the staff members or volunteers offered the prayer. "Thanks for all that have gathered, for the abundance provided, and for the hands that have planted, picked, packaged, and prepared the food." The sincerity and simplicity were so authentic, so unlike the pretentious prayers I had felt obligated to offer to live up to imagined expectations of the pastor being a rhetorician, skilled in the art of speaking to God.

On the first night of my arrival, there was a talent show starting at 7:30, and everyone was invited to participate. It was held in the common room of the Abbey. Though quite spacious, it had a very cozy feel, conducive to making connections with others in the community. As we entered the room, we were greeted by the sight of a fire in the fireplace and a variety of old chairs of various sizes and shapes. I chose a chair that looked like the kind you'd expect to find at your grandparent's home, or perhaps in a church youth room. Next to me was a pleasant-looking young man that I guessed to be in his early twenties, with dark hair and eyes to match.

"Hi, my name is Ralph," I said.

"My name is Abrahan," he responded with an obvious accent.

"I'm from Colorado in the United States. Where are you from?" I asked.

"I am from Paraguay, in South America," he said. At this point, I decided to attempt to bring my Spanish language capabilities, which I had not used for years, back into circulation.

"¿Por que usted está aquí en Iona?" I asked. (Why are you here at Iona?)

"Estoy trato a aprender como a hablar Inglés mejor," he said. (I'm trying to learn how to speak English better.)

"Que bueno," I replied. "¿Hace?" (That's good. How many weeks have you been here?)

"Seis semanas. Sin embargo, estará aquí por seis meses todo." (Six weeks. But I will be here for six months total.)

I don't recall what I said after this, but it was obvious that his ability to speak English was far better than my Spanish. So, we switched back and engaged in further small talk for the short remaining time before the show began.

It was a delightful display of a wide variety of acts and abilities. One person sang light-hearted folk songs while playing their guitar. A small group performed an original and somewhat silly skit they had written, and another person read poetry inspired by the time they had already spent on the island. The showstopper was Margaret, an operatic voice teacher from England, who thrilled us with two outstanding selections. Her voice sounded even more enchanting and heavenly when she sang the Ave Maria in the Abbey chapel service the next morning. The evening entertainment concluded with a terrible tune played on a trumpet by a woman who had never played that instrument before in her life. During that memorable performance, a thought, which would be expanded upon in the weeks to come, was first planted in my awareness: *This place gives people the freedom to be their most vulnerable and authentic selves, not judged for their abilities or lack thereof, but simply accepted as and for who they are.* After a short time of camaraderie and tea, most attendees took a short stroll to the chapel for the evening service.

Every day began and ended with a worship service in the Abbey. Though each service was unique and meaningful in its own rite, this first one was one of the most memorable for me. It was initially a somewhat strange feeling to be in a church setting without having anything to do. As I settled into that holy space, I felt a sense of deep gratitude for the opportunity and freedom to participate in, rather than lead, the service. There was no pressure to perform or assume my pastoral persona to meet the expectations of others. A sense of relief filled me as I sat in the peaceful surroundings, sensing the deep Presence of God in this place.

Winona, one of the staff members, spoke at this service. Her homily was not a carefully crafted treatise meant to convict listeners of sin, criticize culture, or convey a unique theological point. Instead, she told the story of an eagle whose egg was misplaced and hatched among chickens rather than eagles. "As the small eagle grew, it sensed the instinctual urge to fly. When it shared this desire with the other chickens, the eagle was told that it was impossible to do so, as chickens simply couldn't fly. So, the little eagle denied its desire to be who it truly was meant to be and came to believe the misplaced opinions and inaccurate beliefs of the other members of the poultry pen." The message couldn't have been more pertinent. I realized that I also had been attempting to be someone that I wasn't, conforming myself to who I thought I was supposed to be. My exit from ministry was the rejection of that, fleeing from the person I no longer could, or wanted, to be.

As I exited the door, through the cloister, and onto the path back to the MacLeod Center, I paused to take a deep breath. It had been an emotionally, physically, and spiritually overwhelming day that had left me exhausted. Yet I was filled with hope and a sense of optimism instead of discouragement. I realized I had done it! I was at Iona! Years in the making, the journey had finally come to fruition! After only one day, I had gone from feeling like a failure and reject to being welcomed into a caring community. As I settled into my cozy bunk, I found myself reliving the events of this first day, reflecting on the warm words and people who spoke them, and relishing the loving embraces. As I fell off to sleep, I thought about each person I had met. Unwittingly, I omitted one whom I had failed to recognize who was hiding in plain sight: God.

This tiny island was soaked in the Spirit of God. The God present at Iona was different. This was a very old God, having formed that little outcropping at the start of creation. God lingered there even before there were monks and missionaries. God had taken up residence in the ancient Abbey, in the stones lining her walls and floors, and in the huge East Window through which God would peer, at times gazing radiantly in sun rays and shining brilliant light on all the living gathered there. God was sitting in the chairs during the daily services, and on the laps of the guests who came every week. Some recognized this God and felt the Presence, and others were perhaps completely unaware, yet God was certainly there, sitting among them, beside them, and within them! Though it took me a while to recognize it, God was also present in the people I met at Iona. I suspect I didn't realize this because I had been taught that God can only be found in the Word (Bible) and the sacraments (baptism and communion). Yet it quickly became crystal clear that God was hiding in the weary wanderers who made their way to this place, present in the helplessness and hopelessness of their situations, in the shattered dreams which for some had become nightmares. God was not only listening to their prayers, but comforting them as they cried out, oftentimes by sending angels in the form of other people.

The God of Iona brought people out of their troubled spiritual slumbers to live fully awake and walk, striding and skipping joyously into the future. God worked through the staff and volunteers who called Iona home. The Spirit of Iona was very active, evident in their laughter and joy as they carried out their daily duties. God was reaching out to others through them, listening to their prayers, and providing encouragement and comfort, which was expressed so caringly. God was there in the communion that was shared by everyone everywhere, and that was not limited to the scripture read and wine and bread served on Sundays but extended far beyond; in the bread that was broken at meals, the single malt scotch or pint of ale that was partaken of at the pub, in the sacred words shared on a private walk, or in the public gathering at the community hall.

This old God had a very young Spirit, vibrant and vivacious. This Spirit was loving, fun, and fun-loving. This Spirit took great delight in the day-to-day activities that took place, no matter how mundane. This Spirit was pleased, not disappointed, with the people who participated in them, no matter who they were or where they hailed from. This Spirit was not a meek and mild dove, but a wild goose, full of life-giving life. The Spirit of this God was deeply knit into the very fabric of a place and a people unlike any other I'd ever met. This was a holy, unique God living in a wholly unique place.

Of all the introductions at Iona, this one was without doubt the most divine for me. My religious background had fed me a steady diet of distasteful doctrines served up by a God who seemed displeased if one didn't know and follow them. How unexpectedly thrilling to meet the God who was filled with great glee, who rejoices over and in creation, and takes great pleasure in people who were, on the one hand so different from me, and on the other just the same. Mere human beings all struggling with similar challenges and seeking the same thing in life; to be welcomed and loved by others and God.

EIGHT

Loving Community

AND ALL THAT BELIEVED WERE TOGETHER
AND HAD ALL THINGS IN COMMON.
—The Acts of the Apostles

Hospitality was a key component of ancient Celtic culture. The Celts made it a priority to welcome anyone, even strangers, into their communities. It became a bedrock belief in the structure of society and formed the foundation of the first faith communities. This essential component of being united with others in an intimate community was and remains an integral part of daily life. Hospitality is still intentionally practiced in the present day among the Scots. They are, without exception, some of the most hospitable people one will ever meet. Iona rekindled my appreciation for warmth extended to strangers and reminded me of past times where I had experienced something similar.

One event occurred during vicarage, which, in my tradition, took place during the third year of seminary training. The year of vicarage is, in essence, an internship intended to provide a practical learning lab where students can begin to practice what being a pastor entails. In addition, it is meant to serve up a portion of humble pie to rub off some of the rough edges prior to being placed permanently in a parish. I was assigned to a small Spanish-speaking congregation in Del Rio, Texas, a secluded and solitary outpost in the middle of southwest Texas. My supervising pastor was a very kind and gracious man who devoted much of his time and effort to working with the poor across the border in the sister city of Ciudad Acuna, Mexico. At least one day a week, he made a circuit to different homes, some located in the worst of the barrios, leading a Bible study with members of the congregation, their family and friends. On one of our first excursions together, we went to the home of a man named Augustine. He seemed old at the time, though in retrospect, I'm positive the burdens of a life lived in the grinding poverty of the barrio were responsible for his appearance of advanced age. His house was a simple shack consisting of plywood nailed to rough-cut lumber covered here and there with tar paper, and a roof made of rusty corrugated tin. A wooden pallet served as the bottom half of the front door, giving only a poor impression of a barricade. The floor in the house was well-packed dirt. A small wooden table with two green, straight-backed chairs sat in the corner of a small kitchen. It was late August, and the afternoon heat was well over one hundred degrees. It was miserable, and so was I.

With sweat pouring profusely from every pore in my body, I was distracted during the study with comforting thoughts of returning to our air-conditioned vehicle as soon as possible. After what seemed like an eternity, Pastor Greg finally finished the lesson. Relief washed over me as I expected to quickly take leave and find sanctuary in the cool of the truck. Instead, Greg remained seated, carrying on a conversation which I couldn't understand due to my nascent Spanish-speaking abilities, but which soon became clear as Augustine's wife entered the small room carrying a plate of gorditas and three bottles of warm Coca-Cola. As I partook of the spicy fare, prompting an even more prolific outpouring of sweat, and washing it down with the sweet coke, I began to get over myself and my own discomfort, in the process gaining a greater appreciation and admiration for Augustine and his wife, who, out of their poverty, provided so generously for their guests.

Iona was a reminder of occasions like this that I had experienced in the past, but also a reminder of the importance of hospitality and an invitation to put it in the forefront of faith practices. At Iona, I gained a newfound appreciation for the importance of community, and the degree to which it had been lacking. I knew I was lonely as a pastor but didn't realize how much I had been missing until I was thrust into living with others in a true bond of love and fellowship. In ministry, I was surrounded by people, but most of the time felt very alone. I was the leader, not a member of the congregation. Whereas they could act in ways and say things that were acceptable for "regular people," I was held to a higher standard. Seldom did I allow myself the luxury of establishing true friendships as it was difficult to discern who could be trusted. Everyone was an acquaintance. Too often, I felt like the leader of a philanthropic club, or some sort of minor celebrity whose every move is scrutinized. No quarter was given for having a bad day or saying anything other than a kind and encouraging word to or about others. It wasn't just what was said, but how it was said as well. It was a necessity to be pleasant and winsome, no matter what. The effect was to be disingenuous and duplicitous. What a delightful surprise to be received into the Iona Community where honesty and authenticity was the norm, and the health and well-being of the community depended upon it. During the time spent there, I felt as if I was personally experiencing what those first followers of Jesus did after the resurrection when they came together to share one common life and purpose.

Iona allowed me to reflect a great deal upon the role of community in congregations in the U.S. The conclusion I arrived at is that, in large part, congregations reflect the radical individualism of the culture. Practiced and promoted among many clergy, the desire to accumulate more members in their respective congregations has largely replaced foundational principles of the Christian community. It seems as if the ministry model for pastors and congregations can be condensed into three quintessential types.

The first is that of a club. In this model, there are members and non-members, insiders and outsiders, those who belong and those who don't. If you want to belong, you are asked to think, believe, and behave in a certain way. Once one becomes a member, there are levels of membership in which some have more authority than others. Special attention is given to the founding members, who are credited for being the first to build the church. There are also cliques, which sometimes vie for control of the club. The church as a "club" perceives itself as being friendly to visitors and guests, but only those newcomers who are like those already in the club, who reflect or embrace similar values, or who have something of value to offer to the club, whether status, money, musical skills, or a good work ethic, are warmly welcomed. Even now, so long removed from this setting, I'm ashamed to admit that as a pastor, I was not only a part of this club, but I also promoted this model.

The second type is the church as an organization. It might be viewed as a kind of Wal-Mart business model, where the goal is to grow as large as possible. This is done under the guise of "reaching people for Jesus." There is an effective marketing strategy, people being treated like consumers and encouraged to buy into church programs and services. Though appearing to be very friendly and personal, it is a not-so-subtle form of spiritual manipulation. It makes it easy for a person to become lost in the crowd or to surround themselves with other like-minded people in small groups. It reinforces the desire to exercise one's own individualism and personal likes even more fully, as this type of church caters to a wide variety of desires and personal preferences. This model is trendy, and many churches worldwide are emulating it.

At Iona, I was immersed in the third model: the church as community. I believe this is the model that Christ and his followers first practiced, and what the church is intended to be: breathing one Spirit, believing one God, and being one body in which the primary concern is for the well-being of others. The New Testament book of Acts describes the community of these first Christians: "all that believed were together and had all things in common." When people are in community, they celebrate their individuality and diversity while uniting under the One who has called them into being one in Spirit.

At Iona, everyone is welcomed warmly into community, no matter if one is staying a day or a year; whether male or female, young or old, gay, straight, or transgender; no matter where one hails from, be it Europe, Africa, Syria, Canada, Asia, or even the U.S.! The Iona Community exemplifies the words of St. Paul as found in his epistle to the Galatians, "There is neither Jew nor Greek, slave nor free, male nor female, but all are one in Christ Jesus."

At Iona, I encountered other pilgrims who had been judged as living or believing in a wrong way by those who mistakenly believed they'd gotten it right. I felt like one of those pilgrims when I was welcomed into the community. I was welcomed simply for being me. I was, perhaps for the first time in my adult spiritual life, in the presence of others with whom I could feel safe living honestly and authentically as I sought my own true self. I repeatedly contrasted this experience with my former spiritual life, a life spent seeking to satisfy the unrealistic perceptions of others, as well as my own misplaced ideas about what I believed God expected me to be. At Iona, everyone belongs; everyone is embraced, welcomed, accepted, and loved for who they are, not for who they, or others think they ought to be. Inclusivity isn't pontificated from the pulpit, in groups or programs, but rather lived in a humble, quiet, and accepting way. That is to say, in a Christlike way.

At Iona, living in community means not only sleeping in the same room with others, or eating with others at mealtime, but drinking, dancing, praying, working, and playing together. I found that the only way to have time to myself was by getting up early or taking an afternoon walk. Occasionally, the church would be empty late at night, and I could find solitude and solace there. Otherwise, I was surrounded by people all of the time. I liked it that way! The last four years had taught me that I was not good at being alone.

After my father died at a young age, my mom said that the two most difficult times of the day were mealtimes and bedtime. I didn't fully understand what she meant until after my last child left home. It was as if I were living in a museum inhabited by spirits of my past life. Each room held memories, some pleasant and others painful. It felt like the ghosts of my past life were everywhere: in the girls' bedrooms, the den where we celebrated Christmas, and especially in the empty seats surrounding the dining room table, the site of so many family conversations. I would do my best to avoid eating meals alone, which translated into eating on the run or not eating them at all. At Iona, that changed dramatically.

We ate most of our meals together in fellowship. While the din of conversations between forty or fifty people could be distracting, I found it a refreshing change from the silence I had experienced over the past four years. Usually, the conversations that began during mealtimes at Iona continued on long after we had left the dining hall.

One such interaction took place as the result of banoffee pie (a simple delicacy made of banana, cream, and toffee, as the name implies). At dinner one evening, I sat beside three guests from Germany. None of us had ever tasted this delicacy.

"What is this dessert?" One of the German guests asked. "It's quite *delikat*."

"It's called banoffee pie," I told her. "It's a local Scottish delicacy."

"Ah," she said. "How is it made?"

"It has bananas, cream, and toffee."

"Yes," Emma joined in, "It is the best dessert ever. I must learn to make this. You work here. Do you know the cook? Could you get the recipe for us, *bitte*?" she asked.

The Iona Community had a policy against giving out recipes to visitors, only because it would be too demanding to meet the multiple requests of every guest who asked. Nonetheless, wanting to please them, I responded, "Of course I can. I would be happy to work something out for you." I knew that two volunteers working in the kitchen, also from Germany, had an affinity for European chocolate.

"By chance, did you bring any chocolate with you from Germany?" I inquired.

"Yes, of course," said Marlene.

"I think I can broker a deal," I said.

I proceeded to share with them what I was plotting, namely persuading the kitchen volunteers to smuggle me the banoffee pie recipe on the sly in return for European chocolate. Whatever qualms of conscience the kitchen volunteers may have had evaporated after hearing that they could get a fix for their chocolate craving. They discreetly copied the recipe and spirited it out of the kitchen. A pre-arranged meeting place and time was agreed upon with Marlene, Emma, and Adelle, and the next day the exchange was made. All parties were more than satisfied, and the communal spirit of good will was practiced in yet another form.

Some evenings, there would be an informal and impromptu gathering at Martyrs Bay, the local pub. The spirit of togetherness was enriched and enlivened by the spirits of the ale on tap or a good single malt scotch. There's something about the atmosphere of a bar that allows you to be a bit less inhibited. Yes, the "spirits" contribute, but it's more than that. In a church setting, we tend to hide behind a façade. Not wanting to drop our guard, we try to fool others into thinking that we're better than we really are. But in a pub, all pretense is put aside, and we can be ourselves, our exquisitely messy human selves.

I first discovered the value of this atmosphere shortly before leaving for Scotland. An informal group of about eight people began gathering at a small whiskey bar once a week to talk about theology and whatever else was on our minds. We dubbed it "bar church." We were vulnerable and honest with one another. It was a welcome change from the seriousness of the far more sanctified surroundings on Sundays. It was sad to leave that group, and so I was delighted to find a similar setting waiting at Iona.

Though numerous heartfelt conversations were held over a "wee dram" or a pint, there is one that sticks out in my mind. Evening chapel had ended. Abrahan, my supervisor Simon, his partner Linnea, and Rachel, another volunteer, agreed to meet at the pub. As we sat recounting our experiences and what had brought us to Iona, I began to recognize on a deep level that each of us had experienced brokenness in our unique forms. Abrahan's parents had divorced, Simon had been raised by a single mom and had been in a gang, and Rachel was adopted and had experienced the unique challenges associated with that. Each of their experiences had impacted them and the way their lives had played out. Though we had come from different places and were of different ages and backgrounds, our stories contained a common thread: the hurt and heartache that come with being human. The pub provided a safe environment for us to open up, far safer than the church halls had, and prompted us to share those stories. And share we did, not the refined and edited versions, but the uncut ones. The shattered dreams, the unfulfilled hopes, the regrets, and the guilt that naturally accompanied the bad decisions. We freely expressed the pain inflicted by others upon us, as well as the suffering that we had caused others. The brutal honesty of those conversations served as a cathartic confession and formed a spiritually intimate connection between us. It was an experience of human connection more powerful than any I'd ever experienced at a church's altar rail or in a gathering of the sanctified.

I came away from that experience convinced that confession really is good for the soul! My previous church confessions had been perfunctory, prompted by false piety. Twenty-seven years had made me well-practiced at it, but the result was that it provided no personal comfort or consolation. The main result was that it reinforced my false belief that I was actually capable of climbing a spiritual ladder resulting in either religious pride or self-criticism and condemnation when I fell. The type of confession I experienced at the pub was raw and real. We were a table of searching souls responding to an unspoken invitation to bare ourselves, heart and soul, to one another, and in so doing, unwittingly seeking that same type of honesty with God. We opened up to one another, sharing some of our deepest and darkest secrets, the ones we most feared sharing with others, somehow knowing that rather than facing judgment, ridicule, or rejection, we would be accepted and affirmed. The sense of release from ritualistic religiosity and unnecessary requirements granted entrance into an authentic spirituality that was more intoxicating than the Scotch and beer we were drinking! In this unconventional confessional, we were encountering the God that some of us had never known before.

Another locus of community life at Iona was the lounge in the MacLeod Center. With a couch, a couple of old chairs, and a table in the corner, it resembled a combination of a church youth room and a kitschy coffee shop. But it was an excellent place to encounter God, most often in the conversations with others that spontaneously occurred there. It was another safe zone where we could freely talk about our feelings, fears, and faith. It always seemed someone was conversing with another person in the lounge. No matter how busy people were, they always seemed to have time to listen. Perhaps that is how it is with God and our prayers.

God isn't a far-off entity existing way out in the ether of the universe. God is closer to us than we are to ourselves. Prayer is prompted by an awareness of this immanence and takes the form of not inundating God with an endless laundry list of desires or demands, but simply sitting silently to listen to what is being said. It is an opening of the heart and simultaneous emptying of the self so that God can enter in. Or, it is an awareness that God is already there, and one needs only to recognize the Presence. After all those years serving as a pastor, I finally learned to pray at Iona. And in the lounge.

Living in this tight-knit community was instrumental in changing the way I understood God and myself. No longer did I define myself as someone who was "sinful and unclean," as I had confessed on all those pseudo-sanctified Sunday mornings. Now I began to view and accept myself as a beloved child of God, a message I had first read in the writings of Henri Nouwen, black and white words upon a page, which had been translated into living color at Iona. This fundamental change in my perspective not only recast how I saw myself, but how I viewed others. Rather than seeing them as people with problems that needed fixing, I viewed them as people just like me who desired to love and be loved. I realized that I had to love myself well if I wanted to love others. And to do both I had to embrace a loving God who loves all of us as we are, not as we are supposed to be. It's not easy, especially when the message of conditional love is conveyed so clearly not only in culture but in "churchy" congregations. Love becomes dependent on how well you behave, how fervently you pray, how much you give, or how adept you are at pretending to be a committed believer. To arrive at the truth that God loves us just for us is not easy, but when it happens, it is life-changing. Embracing the grace that eliminates expecta-tions or the pressure to live up to a certain standard is transformative. The unconditional, unrestricted, and unbridled love of God was having its way with me via the Celtic spirit of hospitality that was embodied in the lovely and loving people living in the Iona Community.

NINE

Loving Solitude

SILENCE AND SOLITUDE ALLOW US TO MOVE BEYOND THOUGHT
AND INTO OUR EMBODIED EXPERIENCE.
—Frances Weller, *The Wild Edge of Sorrow*

Iona is a secluded place. It is the perfect place to experience sacred silence and practice contemplation. Divine contemplation is a mystical practice, once common to the first monastics, male and female alike, who recognized that to engage meaningfully with the world, one had to disengage and be alone with God. It was quite commonly practiced and widely accepted for many centuries following Christ. The rise of the Reformation and the Enlightenment marginalized the practice, at least in Western mainline Protestantism. Fortunately, the twentieth century witnessed the reappearance and restored appreciation for the practice.

St. Columba and the monastic community he founded recognized the need for solitude and devotedly practiced it. Evidence of this is clearly seen in the remains of the Hermit Cell. Situated a significant distance from the site of the original monastery, it is a modern-day reminder of the importance of separating oneself from others, even in a relatively remote place anyway, to fully participate in sequestered communion with God. This ancient relic reminds pilgrims (especially those with Western sensibilities regarding Christianity) that spiritual solitude was a central tenet of the Celtic Christian community.

These monks were not initiating a novel practice but simply continuing the tradition instituted by Anthony of the Desert and his followers in the third and fourth centuries. *Anthony of the Desert* was a highly influential book written by Anthony's student, Pachomius, and served as the foundation of Christian life. Anthony would be considered eccentric or possibly demented by the standards of today's society. Still, at the time, he was a type of celebrity, leaving society for the sake of seeking God in the serenity of sacred silence. In doing so, he unintentionally led others to follow him into the desert to find God. John Cassian would import these monastic practices from Egypt to Europe in the fifth century and in so doing provide the foundation for monastic communities for centuries to come. Anthony, Columba, Benedict of Nursia, Julian of Norwich, and so many other contemplatives like them recognized the value of what eventually came to be disregarded or discarded after the Protestant Reformation. Recently there has been a rediscovery and renewed appreciation for contemplation. In silence one can be attentive to listening to the voice of God and discerning Divine messages and meaning in life. Intentional solitude nourishes personal participation with the sacred and creates a space to receive epiphanies of Divine mysteries. It also provides an opportunity to process one's emotions, like grief and loss, without interruption. Columba was certainly cognizant of all these benefits, as he frequently practiced contemplation whether on his hill which stands within a stone's throw of the current Abbey, or elsewhere on the island. Though introduced to contemplation previously at St. Walberga and practiced as best I could amid my internal noise and mayhem at the end of my ministry, it was at Iona that I was exposed to a setting ideally suited for quiet contemplation.

Rising early on the second day after my arrival, I went to the north shore to watch the sunrise. Leaving the one-lane road, I passed through a small wooden gate, and followed the narrow path through the pasture, sheep grazing contentedly and occasionally lifting their heads to gaze curiously at the stranger trespassing in their tranquil space. Ascending a small knoll, I came across a bench. It seemed oddly out of place, breaking the natural contour of the terrain, but it seemed to extend an invitation to stop and soak in the serenity of the early morning sunrise. It was as if God had provided a private pew to quietly contemplate the enormity of creation. The water conducted its undulating rhythmic liturgy. The waves broke wildly over boulders by the beach. The cold breeze bent the island grass, delivering the delightful aroma of salty sea air, simultaneously chilling my body while warming my soul. It occurred to me that I was in a natural sanctuary, experiencing the Presence of God. It was a new experience of "church" in which I was invited into the arms of my Divine Lover. The invitation would be extended throughout my time at Iona, and I would be drawn back again and again in the weeks following.

As I sat there in the morning silence, alone with my thoughts, saturated with the sacred, I couldn't help comparing this setting with the one I had just left. It was an uncomfortable feeling to ponder the day ahead of me without making a long mental list of tasks to be accomplished. I could feel the discomfort washing over me as I sat on the bench that first time: "This was a bad decision," I told myself. "I'm not doing anything important here." I thought of the almost hyperactivity that characterized my life before leaving the ministry and coming to Iona. The value I placed on my work and myself was measured in direct proportion to my production and accomplishments. The constant desire for approval and accolades hidden under the thin guise of holy humility was a band-aid for my all-too-fragile ego. This fast-paced lifestyle and desire to merit God's mercy eventually led me to burnout, a condition far too common among clergy.

During my pastoral days, I fell into the trap of personally practicing and at times publicly promoting the idea of sacrificially giving of oneself in service to God. My ministry was defined by achievements, which became the primary way of measuring my self-worth. I expected not only more from myself, but from people in the congregation as well. I was constantly coaxing them to get more involved. I conceived of and implemented events and activities to keep myself and others busy, always preparing, planning, and preoccupied with the next gospel goal. I did this before my divorce, but after my divorce it got worse. If I pushed the pause button on my *doing*, I would be forced to look too deeply into the dark hole in the center of my *Being*. That was the last thing I wanted to do. Externally, I was being rewarded for my avoidance, while inwardly, I was wasting away.

Constantly chasing after spiritual success is inconsistent with the clear examples provided in the scriptures. For the most part, the heroes and heroines of faith were, for all intents and purposes, nothing special, and many were miserable failures. This is true wherever one looks, whether it be at Jacob the deceiver, Jonah the runaway, Jeremiah the weeping prophet, or even Jesus Himself, who died a condemned criminal, abandoned by all but a few. Normal human beings who God uses to accomplish divine purposes in unexpected and even miraculous ways seem to have gone unnoticed in the collective psyche of the modern-day followers of Christ. Motivated by achieving goals and reaching relativistic metrics, there is little room for mediocrity, let alone failure. Current church culture not only highly appreciates, but mandates numerical growth. This number crunching is then used as a measurement of spiritual health and well-being in a congregation or church organization. In the opinion of some in ecclesiastical circles, spiritual health is equated with how many people are joining or attending the services, how much revenue is being generated, and how many programs are being sponsored.

I fell prey to this mentality many times throughout my years in ministry. I wrote monthly reports detailing worship attendance, baptisms and new converts, counseling sessions I'd conducted and the number of visits I'd made to the hospitalized or homebound. It was meant to convince others and myself of the important contributions I was making to the ministry. It helped to justify my worth in their eyes, and by extension God's as well. It was my intention to make others believe that my position was warranted and I was earning my paycheck. It was as if I were trying to impress others with my pastoral performance. This mentality spilled over into my days off. Seldom did I intentionally do nothing. Vacations were spent "going" and "doing" and "seeing" rather than resting, relaxing, and simply being.

This mentality of mine intensified as I faced greater hardships. I believed that the solution to every problem was to double down, to put more effort into resolving whatever the matter was. The congregation in New Mexico had rewarded such efforts. In ten years, I worked hard to grow the church numerically while simultaneously expanding the facilities to accommodate such growth. I oversaw the construction of an addition to the sanctuary, with a new educational wing built to provide space for the parochial school. I didn't take credit for it publicly, but privately, I knew that my abilities and work ethic played a large part in the church's growth. Surely, I thought, such talent would easily translate into similar success at the next parish. I thought wrong.

My hubris resulted in my personal *hamartia* and a hell of my own making. I failed from the very beginning. Under my leadership, the parish lost members, and a preschool sponsored by the congregation closed. I couldn't persuade the church council to pass some of the programs I had proposed. Ultimately, I couldn't successfully hire the personnel I needed to help me save what I saw as a sinking ship. In ten years of ministry in Colorado, my track record was dismal. I doubted myself and my abilities. I blamed myself. Others in the congregation blamed me as well, which transformed my self-doubt into discouragement, despair, and depression. The few positive voices that I heard speaking words of encouragement were not enough to drown out the criticism coming from within, excoriating me for my unworthiness not only as a pastor but as a person as well. Eventually I listened to them. And left.

But leaving that last congregation did not do away with the guilt and shame I felt for being such a failure. I carried those feelings to Iona, where I was confronted with new voices, or sometimes no voices at all, except the voice of God. This is what contemplation accomplishes: the ability to listen to the still, small voice of the Divine.

That morning on the bench was my introduction to a contemplative way of listening, a different way of living, a new way of being. Here, I was able to personally experience the type of spirituality that John Oxenham describes in one of his poems made into a hymn, "Come, occupy my silent place and make Thy dwelling there. More grace is wrought in quietness than anyone is aware." It was there on that bench that I first began to embrace God's silent grace.

In that sacred solitude, the noise of the outside world began to be washed away like the waves that receded into the heart of the sea. Nonetheless, the clamor of the inner cognitive conversations inside my head continued.

I had spent years perfecting my narrative, repeating negative messages, and reminding myself that I was a miserable sinner. Proof for this, I believed, was found in the two areas that mattered most to me: marriage and ministry.

I thought that my divorce egregiously violated two standards that had been impressed upon me throughout my entire pastoral career, the first being the message clearly conveyed in scripture that God ordained marriage,[1] and God hates divorce.[2] The second standard had been set by my parents who had remained married throughout many tough times. I had witnessed firsthand the disappointment of my parents when my oldest sister got divorced, not once but twice. It made me even more determined to make my marriage bulletproof. Deceiving myself into believing that I had done so, I would disdainfully peer upon friends and parishioners whose marriages were, in my opinion, less than stellar and a poor example for what a Christian's marriage should be. In my arrogance, I even openly advocated for clergy who were divorced to be removed from ministry. Like my ego, my marriage was indelible and indestructible, or so I thought.

After my divorce, I spent years examining what had gone wrong. In hindsight, I saw my failures as a husband clearly; I had neglected Pam's needs repeatedly. Granted, I hadn't had an affair, yet I had too frequently abandoned her emotionally and physically to my mistress whose name was "Church." The church and my ministry got the best part of me in terms of both quantity and quality time. Far too often Pam and my daughters were served the leftovers of my love. Too many times she would experience the fallout from my frustration. There were late nights after church council meetings when my disdain for decisions made would be indirectly aimed at her. Over time, serving as the sounding board for my personal and pastoral complaints became too much for her. It was years after the divorce that I came to some clarity and concluded that my wife was tired of living with a complainer and a critic, and she did what she needed to. As I look back, I am surprised it took her so long. And so, I gradually descended into self-loathing for the sorry excuse for a husband I believed myself to be and only realized too late.

---

1 Genesis 2
2 Malachi 2:16

The bench on the north beach provided the first place where I could intentionally practice the refining process of doing away with all those painful memories and regrets. It wasn't the only one, as a few days later, I was invited again into the quiet and contemplative solitude of the Machair.

On my first trip to Iona I had learned of St. Columba's Bay, the location where he had purportedly first landed. That became my destination a few days later. Immediately following my midday duties, I was determined to make my way to that bay. On the way I came to the Machair, a long expanse of meadow-like land that had once been used to grow crops and vegetables but now served the double duty of a pasture upon which the sheep grazed, and part of the rough island golf course. From a distance the crashing waves caught my eye. I was drawn to the sight of the violent collision of the waves upon the beach, and the sound of the pounding surf. I approached the edge of the meadow, where it dropped off into sandy bluffs that looked out over the sea and led down to the rocky beach below.

Carefully picking my path down to the beach, I slowly walked out onto a narrow, rocky peninsula that thrust me into the midst of the surf, having the effect of making me feel as if I were a participant rather than a bystander. There I stood for quite some time, engulfed in the sound of crashing silence, even amid such magnificently loud surroundings. In the same way the waves broke upon the beach, so too the immensity of what and Who surrounded me broke over me. I was carried away, overwhelmed by my own insignificance compared to the grandeur of the Creator of heaven and earth. It was a moment of vulnerability and weakness. And yet, it was simultaneously strangely consoling, as I contemplated the comfort that comes from being in such close communion with creation. As I looked over the vast expanse of ocean wilderness, the words of Psalm 8 came to mind, "What is mankind that Thou are mindful of us?"

It was then, immersed in deep thought and simple prayer, that God revealed to me the reason that I had been guided to Iona. It wasn't really to escape ministry, start a new life, or even to rest and relax, though all of these were part of the picture. Rather, it was simply to *Be*. To be still. To be someone and something other than who and what I thought I was. To be with God, and for God to be with me. Strange how the soul, body, and mind are brought into harmony with the Divine when freed from the concerns and constraints of everyday life. In those moments, I felt as if I was one with my surroundings, with nature, with God. I luxuriated in the experience of being lost in the love that was around and within me.

I don't know how long I stood there on that promontory, soaking in those sacred surroundings. After a time I carefully retreated from the outcropping and returned to the beach to sit on the bluff, still lost in the undulation of the waves, lulled into a place that caused me to reflect on my life in the years immediately preceding my arrival at Iona.

I saw myself as having become a shipwreck, having been washed up on the beach at Iona in the hopes that from the debris a new life could be rebuilt. For that to happen I needed forgiveness, a theological concept that I had frequently preached about, but for the most part failed to personally practice. Intellectually, I knew that forgiveness was a tenet of my faith, but it was a gift I seldom bestowed upon myself. Foremost was my inability to forgive myself for what had happened to mom. She had died three years earlier of Alzheimer's disease. It was an ongoing battle to find peace amid the guilt over how her last years had transpired. I regretted how the end of her life played out and the part I played in it. I had failed her in her hour of need.

I had been given numerous chances to serve congregations in Wisconsin and be near her; once in 1990 while serving in Chicago, another time in 1995 after returning from Papua New Guinea, and the third time in 2004 while living in Las Cruces. On each occasion, I chose to go elsewhere. She was left to personally experience her own "Zebedee Moment." He was the father of James and John, who was left behind as his sons abandoned him to follow Jesus. My spiritual arrogance, masquerading as faithful zeal, was motivated by pride and self-centeredness. The realization of how she must have felt didn't fully hit me until I, too, was left alone. When I walked into my big, empty house after depositing my youngest daughter at college, the enormity of what it must have been like for Mom hit home. I was by myself. No one was there for me, just as I had not been there for my mother. My dear, sweet mother. As I sat there, I recalled all the ways I had failed her:

I wasn't there for her when Dad died. Too consumed with my own career and family, I failed to appreciate the great loss she was experiencing and respond accordingly.

After living with her for six months after our return from PNG, I failed to consider how lonely she would be when we left for our latest venture in Las Cruces.

When she was diagnosed with Alzheimer's disease, I didn't take the initiative to be near her, to walk with her on this horrible journey.

And as she took her last breath, I was absent again, as I had been so many times before. Even though she had always been there for me.

My many failures morphed into regrets, the regrets into guilt, and the guilt into shame. I had failed my mother repeatedly.

As I sat on that beach replaying the record of my regrets for the millionth time, I heard another voice speaking to me. It was a gentle voice, barely audible over the crashing of the waves. "It is time to forgive yourself. I forgive you. That's who I Am. Your mother forgives you. That's who she is. Let my loving grace wash over you and carry the rubble of your guilt and regret into the sea. Allow My Spirit, who hovered over the waters in the first creation and who is hovering over these waters, wash and renew your spirit. Your mother is with Me and I am with you. She is not far away." At that moment, I believed. Fully. And I received in my innermost being the gift of forgiveness. The forgiveness I was dying for was not found in the pages of a book, nor spoken by rote in a religious worship service, or even by another person, but by the Spirit of the living God, who is the God of the living.

In those moments of deep contemplation, I experienced a huge step on the path to transformation. The Spirit was present, as it had been in those primordial waters, providing resuscitation, restoration, and forming me into a new creation. Just at that moment, my eyes fixed upon a seashell. In my religious tradition, the seashell symbolizes baptism, the bestowing of new life. Mom loved walking along beaches on vacation and collecting shells. As I gently grasped this heavenly gift, I was mindful of the gift of my mom, the life she had first given me, and the new life of forgiveness into which I was now being delivered. Now it was time to live that life of forgiveness.

That gift was what I contemplated as I crossed the Machair and walked back toward the village. God had given me an enormous gift on the bench, and the beach, just the first of many I would receive while in contemplation at Iona.

TEN

Loving Celebration

LET THEM PRAISE HIS NAME IN THE DANCE.
—Psalm 149

As a child, Sundays were reserved for church ... and dancing. After enduring what seemed like an eternity spent in the purgatorial experience of an old Lutheran pastor's preaching, we would hurry home and quickly change out of our Sunday best. Awaiting us was not only the big Sunday meal that Mom was preparing but "polka time" featuring Frankie Yankovich or Alvin Styczynski, the musical maestros of our small world. By turning on our black and white Zenith TV, our small living room space was transformed into our own little dance hall. My four sisters, older than me by between four and fourteen years, would take me in their arms and twirl me around in time to those oompah-pah polka tunes or have me stand on their feet so that I could learn the waltz. Amidst the revelry, my father somehow managed to read the Sunday paper while my mother put the finishing touches on the feast, usually consisting of roast beef, mashed potatoes, carrots, green beans, or peas, with a homemade pie or cake for dessert. Unlike the Methodists or Baptists, we Lutherans embraced dancing. And drinking. Lots of drinking.

There were opportunities to do so at an occasional 4-H gathering or barn dance, but the most common venue was weddings. Wisconsin weddings were a cause for a grand and glorious celebration that didn't end until the wee hours of the morning. A large group of our family and friends would join us for the festivities. I remember a cornucopia of food served buffet-style, the beer flowing like water from the tap, and a lot of dancing. All those post-church polka dance parties prepared me well for the wedding celebrations of friends, relatives, and eventually my sisters' weddings. Sunday services seemed to flow seamlessly into celebrations. I came to the conclusion that while God might tolerate a long, boring church service, it was certain that God considered a dance celebration divine.

Scripture confirms this truth. If you look carefully, you can see and hear God celebrating throughout the Christian scriptures. In the book of Genesis, an effervescent God dances over the dark waters, singing all things into being. Just listen to the rhythms: the sun begins to shine, the moon begins to glow, flowers bloom, grass grows, rain falls, birds sing, cattle bawl, and all creation breaks forth in the first cantata. As a divine encore, humans are formed from the primordial loam, created in the image of God, to reflect, radiate, and rejoice in the beauty of being alive. God is both composer and conductor in that first cosmic symphony. It is a performance that continues unabated, both inviting and compelling all things to join in the universe's ongoing *opus magnum*.

In Christ, the divine dance came fully to life in human form. According to the Gospel records, His birth is announced by a choir of angels singing a heavenly Hallelujah Chorus. Others who see Him, like Zechariah, sing as well. Not to mention His own mother who breaks forth into her song of praise, called The Magnificat, at the announcement of the child in her womb, who brings life to the whole world. Is it any surprise that the first miracle recorded in the Gospel of St. John was turning water into wine at a wedding? On more than one occasion Jesus describes heaven not as a worship service, but as a wedding banquet.

It is easy to imagine Jesus dancing. Shirking sour and dour religiosity, He frequently approached life with joviality, much of His ministry serving as a litany punctuated by laughter and light-heartedness. He utilized stories of celebrations, such as the great wedding feast or eschatological banquet, to illustrate the true nature of God and the never-ending jubilation and exultation that God has for all creation. The Prodigal Son, one of His most familiar and best-loved stories, is about a father welcoming his long-lost son home and feting him with extravagant festivities. Even knowing of His imminent death, Jesus celebrated with a Passover banquet. His followers may not have gotten it initially, but they certainly did after His resurrection. We see them filled with joy, their hearts burning as they gathered regularly to rejoice in their new lives and the anticipation of seeing Him again.

I have a painting in my home that captures this kind of Christ, entitled *The Smiling Jesus*. In this portrait, Jesus isn't the Suffering Servant spoken of by Isaiah, somberly praying in the Garden of Gethsemane, or dying the gruesome and garish death on a cross. Instead, Jesus' face, slightly weathered, is glowing with a bright, wide smile. This is not a subtle, Mona Lisa-like smile, but one fully formed, as if He had just heard or told a joke. Perhaps the Jesus depicted here is preparing for a party or already participating in one. Maybe this is how He looked at the children before gently placing them in His lap, at the people with leprosy before healing them, and as He watched the multitudes enjoy the meal He provided.

This is the God I had been introduced to by my parents and sisters, who had eluded the sanctimonious scruples of so many church-going people. The "don't drink, smoke, swear, or dance" prohibition had been partially set aside by my mother, and fully forgotten by my father. They had raised me in a not-too-strict form of religion. But in time, that changed. Attending a conservative Lutheran college and seminary, I was introduced to the more serious side of religion. Sanctification, a word interpreted to mean "living a holy life," for me took on the interpretation of "Take this God stuff more seriously." Gradually, in the quest to be a good candidate for becoming a pastor, the delightful dance I had experienced in my formative years was replaced by a far-too-sanctimonious belief system. I was taught that the business of God is serious business, and left little time for celebration, especially in church.

St. Irenaeus said, "The glory of God is man fully alive." Ever so slowly, the magnificence of God I had once experienced in being fully alive was obscured by the solemn veil of sacred pursuits. The direction of my life was dictated by the desire to please God through the overly serious practice of pastoral ministry. I was happy to celebrate birthdays, holidays, and other special occasions when I wasn't in the church environment. But when I assumed my pastoral role, the practice of religion became serious business.

All that changed at Iona. I was reintroduced to a freedom of spiritual expression that had been long since forgotten. There were unexpected and surprising reasons to celebrate every day. Sometimes it was when we joyously departed the Abbey at the end of a worship service, dancing as we left. At other times it was while savoring a warm cup of tea in the presence of another person in the lounge, watching rain dance across the windowpanes, or frolicking in the Presence of God as we splashed and swam on the North End beach. It all was cause for exultation. Joy was found in being fully present with a light and loving spirit, enjoying what was being done and who it was being done with and for.

As time went on, I found that I could appreciate these little daily life celebrations that I had previously overlooked. In the mornings, I became less consumed with doing the ritual of my daily devotions in a regimented way, less concerned with what tasks needed to be checked off my to-do list, and began to give space to whatever was presented to my awareness. It became a time of communion that was more a celebration than an obligation.

Celebrations materialized both spontaneously and as the result of regularly scheduled times set aside for just such a purpose. One of the weekly highlights was the Monday night Ceilidh. The Ceilidh, which means "companion" in Gaelic, is a traditional Irish festivity comprised of song, dance, and storytelling. After the evening service, staff and guests walked to the Village Hall, a small, old, stone building. Its charmingly simple appearance and atmosphere extended a warm welcome on so many chilly Scottish nights. A few small benches lined three of the walls. A table sat in the corner near the small kitchen, which served as the repository for biscuits and "squash," a Scottish cordial. A small and simple stage, elevated a few feet above the main floor, provided the place for a person or group to perform.

The Village Hall reminded me of the stage and dance hall at the North Star Pavilion, where I grew up in Wisconsin. It was a popular setting for wedding receptions, and it was where our 4-H club joined with kids from other clubs to square dance during the long Wisconsin winters. Both village halls had a unique smell of aged wood treated with floor wax. Those types of places are long gone, unfortunately replaced by more modern facilities. When I walked into the old Village Hall at Iona, it was as if I had been transported back to my childhood. It gave me goosebumps.

The weekly Ceilidh performances consisted of Celtic music and mirth. Sometimes, a small band would take the stage; at other times, there would be a solo act playing the Irish flute or performing a piece that reflected the place they hailed from. A person might tell a story or recite a poem. It all depended on what guests were there that week. The acts were as diverse as the people who had come to Iona.

One night, I joined the act called "St. Columba and the Vikings." Sung to the tune "Mama Mia" by ABBA, it was a song recounting an imaginary meeting between the Norseman and Columba. Simon had dug up some plastic Viking helmets from one of the storage closets, so we put them on and donned other garments that served as a poor but effective imitation of what the invaders wore. In the spirit of fun and creativity, we enlisted a young female volunteer to play the part of Columba. The song ended with our Columba being carried off the stage by the four Vikings. The act went so well that there was a request for an encore performance.

The mainstay of the evenings was the dancing, which was somewhat like those square dances I went to as a kid, set to Celtic music. The evening would usually start slowly, many guests unfamiliar with the music and dance moves. The staff and volunteers would break the ice by being the first to take the floor, and then good-naturedly grab hold of those who were reticent to join in. The guests soon learned that you didn't have to be a good dancer or know the steps to enjoy the Ceilidh; you could leave your inhibitions behind and lose yourself in the gaiety. It didn't take long for them to release all their reservations. Soon, the dance floor was filled with "Lord of the Dance" wannabes. The Ceilidh would last for almost two hours, with a short break in the middle to allow everyone to partake in refreshments and conversation. All too soon, the night's final song, "Whip the Willow," would be played. It seemed like a more exuberant form of the Virginia Reel, with trios of people clasping arms and flinging one another in turn in tight circles. The exuberance on display was boundless and unbridled. The evening came to an end too quickly, and we left the village hall in small groups, our sweaty bodies met by the cold and moist Scottish weather, making for a very brisk walk back to our lodgings. There, the reflections on the day would often last until well into the wee morning hours.

When each day is a celebration, the "small things" get bigger, and the "big things" get a bit smaller. Take the Fourth of July, for example. Iona didn't officially celebrate it, which was fitting, considering the Fourth of July wasn't a celebration of Scottish independence. It was odd not to have fireworks, parades, or barbecues. Some of the U.S. citizens decided to have some sort of simple celebration. We gathered at the jetty where we kicked off the festivities by pouring a pot of tea into the water, no doubt making our forefathers proud. Our little re-enactment of the Boston Tea Party was followed by the singing of a few familiar patriotic songs and then the national anthem. The ceremony ended with a short prayer and the pledge of allegiance. Our little celebration lacked the grandiose and glorious trappings of a fireworks display or citywide parade. Still, for us it was a special little moment that had great significance. Out of all the Independence Days I've celebrated in my life, this one is the most memorable. On the way back from the jetty, we discussed how thankful we were for the place we came from but also how appreciative we were of Iona and the opportunity we had there to meet so many people who were also thankful for the places they hailed from and called home. Passing the SPAR convenience store, we stopped in to get a Coke and some chips, putting the finishing touches on a very American celebration of the Fourth of July.

The jetty was the site of numerous celebrations. Volunteers and guests were first welcomed at the jetty as they set foot on the island, many for the first time. The volunteer coordinator and a small delegation of volunteers always met them. The volunteers were constantly turning over, some arriving and others leaving every week. And yet, it didn't stop us from forming deep friendships. You get to know others quickly, skipping formalities and small talk and diving right into the most vulnerable parts of their lives. You could only spend a few days with someone and feel like you'd known them your whole life. It made saying goodbye difficult. The jetty served as the place to bid farewell as others boarded the ferry that would conduct them back to the "real" world. Iona provided the hope and healing that my fellow pilgrims had sought. It was from the jetty that we would watch the ferry recede toward the far shore, returning those leaving to their former lives, which for most would never be the same.

One more celebration demands mentioning—the games we played. Every Thursday night following our volunteer meetings, we would gather to play games. These were not board games but rather games that demanded full-body participation. The blanket game was a consensus favorite. Four people would stand on a blanket, and then begin folding it, attempting to keep all four team members on the blanket as it got progressively smaller. I teamed up with Liam, Kristina, and Catherine on one occasion. Liam was a hefty young man who hailed from Glasgow and had the build of a rugby player. As we folded the blanket and the space became smaller and smaller, we began forming a human pyramid of sorts. Liam was standing upright, holding me in his massive arms. Kristina was clinging to my back, and Catherine was somehow hanging from the three of us like a monkey in a tree. The pose was short-lived, and we fell to the floor in a heap, laughing hysterically.

Another favorite Thursday night game was a form of modified musical chairs. In this version of the game, participants were not allowed to touch the ground. We'd walk on the chairs, sit down, or attempt to when the music ended. Inevitably, people would be sent flying to the floor. It was a minor miracle that no one was injured.

Iona served as a powerful reminder of the simple joy found in being a child of God. At Iona, I was reintroduced to the God who laughed, danced, and didn't take religion too seriously. At Iona, I relived what Sundays were like as a child. At Iona, the weight of trying to bear up under the burden of far-too-heavy religiosity was removed from my shoulders and replaced by wings which made it much easier and more enjoyable to celebrate with laughter and dancing. Forever Dancing.

ELEVEN

Loving Worship

ON IONA WE ARE COMMITTED TO THE BELIEF THAT WORSHIP
IS EVERYTHING WE DO, BOTH INSIDE AND OUTSIDE THE CHURCH.
—*The Iona Abbey Worship Book*

Iona is an island whose very fabric seems to sing. Praise sounds forth from the sea and land, reaching into one's very soul. If paying attention, music and songs seem to come from everywhere on Iona. Here things are in tune; there is a natural harmony and rhythm to the island that breathes life into the soul. The song of Iona achieves its crescendo in and around the Abbey. Every day begins and ends with a worship service in the sanctuary, when the bells of this grand old dame call out the invitation to graciously gather and receive the gifts of God given in worship.

The previous Abbey had been constructed in the thirteenth century by Benedictine monks and then destroyed during the Protestant Reformation. Over the centuries the local population pilfered the stones, using them for more practical purposes like building homes and walls. For hundreds of years, all that remained were the scattered remnants of what was once one of the most significant religious sites in Western Christendom. In 1938, a Church of Scotland pastor named George MacLeod, who had witnessed firsthand the horrors of World War I and, as a result, became a pacifist, was inspired to rebuild the ancient edifice. He recognized during the years of the Great Depression the need to impart hope and healing to the many who were void of both. At the time, he served in a very poor part of Glasgow called Govan. During a pilgrimage to Iona, he received his epiphany to undertake a resurrection of the Abbey as the focal point for a new ecumenical community committed to peace. Not only would it mean work for some of the unemployed craftsmen, but it would also provide a place where the message of the Prince of Peace, the Shar Shalom, could be proclaimed to a world badly shaken and trying to move out of the dark shadows of world war. The present-day structure is not only a tribute to MacLeod's ingenuity and persistence, but also a symbol of his unrelenting desire to restore and rebuild lives, one stone at a time.

Other magnificent buildings found in the world that have been constructed to the glory of God are more architecturally impressive than the Iona Abbey. But something is unique in this building that takes one beyond the mere artistic and architectural abilities of mankind. There is something different that transcends time and space, as if the island itself and the spirits that reside here animate the building. Perhaps it is the Spirit who guided the first monks from Ireland. Perhaps it is the spirits of those who worshiped on this site for so many centuries, the spirits of those who rebuilt it, or maybe the spirits of the present-day saints who belong to the Iona Community. Maybe it is all these combined. Whatever it is, it embodies what the Celts called a "thin place," a place where heaven and earth intersect.

Most of those who enter the Abbey do so from the west through massive wooden doors. They are greeted first by the baptismal font, which is made of green Iona marble. Stone steps lead down to the long aisle, flanked by row upon row of wooden chairs. This part of the church, called the nave, leads to another section, traditionally called the choir; two long, ornate, wooden structures with individual seating face each other across the aisle. To the immediate left is the elevated dais that provides the place from which the person leading the service stands. The aisle culminates at the chancel, the raised stone platform upon which a large altar, also made of Iona marble, stands in simple majesty. It is a massive flat stone tablet that, to some, might bring to mind the altar Aslan was bound to in C. S. Lewis's *The Lion, the Witch, and the Wardrobe.* The East Window rises above the chancel, shedding light upon those gathered within the walls of the Abbey.

Traditionally, churches were intentionally constructed in the shape of the cross and faced the east, the direction of the rising sun, a reminder of the rising of God's Son. The East Window serves as a prism for the sunshine at Iona, rare though it may sometimes be, to shine on weary pilgrims sitting in the various shades of their own personal shadows. This is the sacred setting that serves as the locus for the life of worship at Iona.

Worship is not merely a part of life at Iona, it *is* life. At Iona, the service that is given to others flows into and out of the doors, emulating the ocean's movement on the island's shores. There is neither an invocation to start worship nor a closing benediction, conveying the subtle message that there is no beginning and no end, that worship is part of everything one does, part of everything one is. No stark distinction separates the "secular" and the "sacred," holy and profane, church and life. Worship provides a subtle daily reminder of the faith of the Celtic Christians who saw God always active in all things, and, therefore, was to be praised and prayed to every-where and always.

The morning service begins with the reminder, "The world belongs to God." To which everyone responds, "The Earth and all its people."[1] A confession of sorts follows this opening, but one that was drastically different from the type of confessions I had known. My former church confession called me to join with others in claiming to be "sinful and unclean" and "justly deserving God's present and eternal punishment." No wonder I loathed myself! I was left asking myself, "How could I ever be good enough to please others, let alone God?" Too often, I was filled with a sense of shame and guilt at the beginning of those services, an effect that I am certain I shared with many others. The sins that most burdened me were not the ways in which I had transgressed the commandments or violated God's laws. Rather, the cause of my consternation was constantly being reminded of my sinfulness, my worthlessness, and my failures both as a pastor and person. It wasn't the multiplicity of my personal peccadillos that most grieved me, but rather the duplicity and inauthenticity that came

---

1 This quote and all that follow are found in The Iona Community, *The Iona Abbey Worship Book* (Glasgow: Wild Goose Publications), 2002.

from playing the part of a person I no longer recognized, and, in fact, had never been. I suffered most from the sin of what I call Pharisaical phoniness, an affliction all too common among clergy. We assume a false identity, pretending to be someone that we're not, in the hopes of becoming more sacred and less sinful than those we're supposed to be serving. For me, the weight of this play-acting resulted in a serious case of mistaken identity, exchanging who I really was for who I thought I should be.

The confession at Iona provided soothing salve for my sick spiritual condition. Rather than worthlessness, it spoke of woundedness. In lieu of a denunciation and subtle threat of damnation, it offered a gracious invitation.

"Before God, with the people of God, I confess to my brokenness; to the ways I wound my life, the life of others, and the life of the world."[2]

The confession at Iona invited authenticity and vulnerability rather than eliciting shame and guilt. Instead of flagellating and beating a person down, these words built up. The words of healing that followed furthered the effect.

"May God forgive you; Christ renew you; and the Spirit enable you to walk in love."[3]

This confession was followed by prayers for God's help and the Lord's Prayer, which was slightly modified, reading "Save us in the time of trial" in place of "Lead us not into temptation."[4] I found this to be less confusing and easier to apply to everyday life. Rather than giving the impression that God could and would capriciously lead us into any type of temptation, the revised version assured us that in the midst of life's many trials, God rejoiced in rescuing us.

After the prayers came the Affirmation of Faith. In my tradition, this would've been one of the historic creeds: the Nicene or the Apostles. But here it read as follows:

2 *Worship Book*, 16
3 *Worship Book*, 17
4 *Worship Book*, 17

Leader:	With the whole church
All:	We affirm that we are made in God's Image,
	befriended by Christ, empowered by the Spirit.
Leader:	With people everywhere
All:	We affirm God's goodness at the heart of humanity,
	planted more deeply than all that is wrong.
Leader:	With all creation
All:	We celebrate the miracle and wonder of life;
	the unfolding purposes of God, forever at work
	in ourselves and in the world.[5]

The first time I spoke these words, one of the false cornerstones of my previous religious convictions crumbled. I was taught that the image of God, in which human beings were originally created, had been completely lost because of Adam and Eve's fall into sin. The consequence was that their descendants, all of us, were born as horrible human beings, completely infected with the "disease" of sin, which defined who we were and determined how God viewed us. In my tradition, Psalm 51, with its penitential prose, provided the proof text for our personhood, "Conceived in sin and shapened in iniquity."

To fully appreciate love and grace, I was taught in my Lutheran tradition that one had to become completely cognizant of how horribly marred and misshapen we are, and then sincerely repent … and repent … and repent. Without sincere sorrow, one couldn't receive nor fully appreciate forgiveness. Of course, one could never be certain that they were adequately sorry or sufficiently sincere to merit this divine mercy. Even though it was presented as being biblical and thoroughly Christian, the truth was that this doctrine transformed God from a loving Father into a terrible taskmaster or worse, an eternal torturer. Over time, this doctrine had a debilitating effect on me. No matter how hard I tried, I could never live up to God's expectations. I became more critical of myself and, in an attempt to deflect

---

5 *Worship Book*, 17.

my guilty conscience, more critical of others. This teaching was toxic to me, and I'm certain to many others over whom it was pronounced.

At Iona, I began to believe that it wasn't Psalm 51 that defined one's humanity, but rather Psalm 139, which speaks of us being wonderfully made by a loving God who knit us together in our mother's wombs. Just like Jesus! Each morning service reminded me that sometimes, our failures are just part of the human condition, they don't render us unworthy of God's love. Instead of hearing about sin and its punitive consequences, those gathered were reminded over and over that each person is so much better than the worst thing we'd ever done. We were not horrible human beings as we'd been led to believe, but precious and dearly loved children of God.

As that new realization began to seep through my hard outer shell and into the darkest recesses of my spiritual soul, I experienced a personal epiphany. I became acquainted with a God who knows me better than I know myself and loves me not despite my humanity but because of it! This God is a lover, not a hater. This God looks with wonder and awe upon all of creation and loves it and us! This God does not set impossible standards to live up to, but rather stoops down to be with us in the midst of the murky mess that is life. This God is kind and compassionate and views each person through the light of divine love.

The light that streamed through the East Windows accentuated this truth and illuminated not only the Abbey but the dark recesses of my soul. God was speaking a different language. One filled not with criticism and condemnation, but with comfort and consolation. God was speaking this message not only in the words of the worship leader, but through the warm embrace of the person sitting next to me, in the hands extended in love to strangers, in the arms raised in prayer, and in the voices filled with song. These songs rejoiced in the gift of receiving God's love.

The message of the love of God was also heard in the prayers. They were simple prayers meant to be expressed to God with humility, sincerity, and familiarity, as though the God being prayed to was not only transcendent but immanent as well. I found those said at the conclusion of each morning service, especially the ones on Friday, the most meaningful. On that day of leaving, all those gathered would pray this petition for God to take us outside of the ancient walls, and outside of our own experience of "holiness" into the crossroads of the world "where soldiers curse and nations clash."[6] Living as secluded saints seeking to be sequestered in a safe and far-away place was not sufficient. The Iona Community called us to step forth in faith from the safety of the sacred sanctuary and engage with others, doing the work of God in the world. The closing sentences of the morning service beckoned us to go forth and serve God's loving purpose to live together in community, another form of worship, to work, eat, laugh, play, and pray, occasionally by ourselves but more often with others. Twelve hours later, we would again be drawn back by the bells to bring closure to the day.

Regardless of which service it was, people were welcome to come as they were. For some, me included, that meant wearing stocking caps to keep warm in that old stone church. Wearing whatever kept you warm became kind of a custom, and no one seemed to care. No one at Iona, that is. Shortly after leaving Iona, I was reminded that the divine dress code was still enforced elsewhere. At Glasgow Cathedral, I entered wearing my stocking cap. A steward kindly requested that I remove my head covering. I was struck by the irony that, evidently, it was more of an affront to God to be wearing a cap than it was for them to be selling souvenirs in the vestibule of that very sacred space. I was reminded of the scene where Jesus drives the money changers out of the temple. At Iona, there was no need to dress to impress, and there was no concern that what one wore disqualified a person from being accepted by God. What a difference this was from what I had experienced in my previous ecclesiastical life.

In my upbringing, wearing "Sunday go-to-meeting" clothes was important. Dressing up for God was a given. It was like preparing to meet a dignitary. I carried that mentality with me into ministry. Elders were expected to wear suits. If they were assisting with the worship service, they were to wear a white robe, like mine. The acolytes, adolescent-aged children

---

6 *Worship Book*, 21.

who were taking classes in preparation for confirmation, also wore white robes. They went through special training that taught them the routine of lighting the candles, picking up the communion cups, and the importance of appropriate attire. Dress shoes were required. On one occasion, I refused to allow a young man to carry out his assigned duties simply because he showed up wearing tennis shoes. I had conveyed the message that God cared more about the apparel that adorns the outside than the spirit that dwells within.

The first Christmas after returning from Iona, I surprised my family by attending the Christmas Day service wearing my Iona hooded sweatshirt. If God could appear on Christmas wearing swaddling clothes, I told myself, certainly, I could show up in a sweatshirt. The divine informality at Iona was the practice of religion with a relaxed feel, similar, I believe, to what Jesus valued and embodied.

Not so in the sanctuaries I served in and the worship services I presided over as a pastor. Both presented a challenge to anyone who hadn't been born and bred in the stable of Lutheranism. I sympathized with those spiritual seekers who would sometimes wander through the doors uncertain of what they would find, only to have their confusion compounded as they were subjected to a style of religious ritual that required endless page flipping and popping up and down in one's pew, performing pious calisthenics. The challenging tunes to some of the traditional Lutheran hymns, the seriousness and sobriety of the service, the "unwelcome" extended at the time of communion, and the frequently less-than-friendly reception that they received resulted in not a few guests fleeing following the service never to return.

When I arrived at Iona, the tables turned on me. I was now the one being challenged and at times made uncomfortable in worship, not for the difficult obstacles it presented but for the delight, not for the seriousness but the spontaneity, not for feeling as if the doors were closed to guests, but that they were opened wide.

Those doors also opened wide each night for the evening service. Whereas the morning services were quite similar, following essentially the same pattern, the evening services were each very different, having a unique theme.

Sunday night was a quiet, contemplative service. No music, no responses, only a simple reading. It was in the form of the ancient practice of *lectio divina*. After a scripture reading, everyone sat for a half hour of intentional silent meditation. Immediately following was the Taizé service conducted by volunteers. A favorite of guests and staff alike, the Taizé service spotlighted the different languages and cultures represented on the island.

The service of Peace and Justice was held on Monday evening. It was a reminder that the Old Testament style of retributive justice was a far cry from the restorative justice of the Loving God alive in the first followers of Jesus. The themes were as diverse as recycling cell phones, to healthy eating, to supporting equitable and Godly political efforts in places like the Middle East. Essentially, it was a call for loving forgiveness, rather than hate-driven retribution.

Tuesday night was the service of healing. The service had three parts: The first recognized volunteers leaving the following day. The director would call their name, have them stand, and then speak a parting blessing intended just for them. The second part included lengthy prayers for people whose names had previously been placed into the prayer request box. The last part consisted of inviting those in attendance to come forward for a personal prayer of healing. There was a small circle, so significant in Celtic faith and culture, consisting of nine kneeling pads. Inside the circle were three staff members or volunteers. Those gathered would be invited to come forward and, upon kneeling, would have hands placed upon their heads as the following was prayed over them, "Spirit of the Living God, present with us now, enter your body, mind, and spirit and heal you of all that harms you. In Jesus' Name. Amen."[7]

Here was another novel element to worship that had been foreign in my experience. Lutherans believe that the gift of direct healing, common in the New Testament, had ended with the Apostles. Suspicion, and at times even

---

7 *Worship Book*, 91.

derision, was cast at those religious traditions that adopted direct healing as a present-day practice. I remembered a girl I dated in high school who believed in "charismatic Christianity." I attended a healing revival with her that was more like a staged religious production. The pastor theatrically claimed to be imbued with the gift of healing. People fell on the ground as he spoke, writhing around in spiritual ecstasy. I was so disturbed by that experience that I couldn't bear to go again, no matter how much I liked that girl! But this service was different. This was a quiet and contemplative occasion based on the belief that God already knows where and how we hurt, and desires for us to be healthy and whole. A palpable sense of peace filled me throughout the service as I sat in quiet meditation. This was true healing.

One day, as we were working together in the kitchen, Brenda, a volunteer, came to me with a request that I wasn't ready for.

"Would you like to take part in the healing service this week?"

"I'm really not comfortable doing that," I replied.

"That's good," she said, "God leads us out of our comfort zone, and that's where growth takes place."

"I have experienced a great deal of growth here already," I said.

Without missing a beat, she replied, "That's wonderful! This will provide an opportunity for you to share that with others."

I couldn't think of a reason to say no, so I reluctantly agreed.

Reading the names of those we were praying for was simple. But then came the time for me to stand in the circle. I placed hands on people as we said the prayer. It was both humiliating and exhilarating, as I simultaneously recognized the working of the Spirit while battling against my doubts, cynicism, and skepticism. In the end, I did my best to get out of the way and let God work. My hands felt warm a couple of times, though I'm unsure if that was due to the Spirit or my nervous perspiration. As people came forward, I felt a weight lift off of my shoulders. It was my own healing that I was experiencing. This sense of well-being remained with me long after that service.

Wednesday was the Agape Service. Agape, which means love, was the name first given to what came to be known as the Eucharist by the first followers of Christ. The Abbey was dark, dimly illuminated for the most part only by candles. There was a long table in the center aisle. The celebrant, an ordained female staff member, was sitting at the head of the table. She began the service with great solemnity, reminding us that this was a service of love. And thus, the intent was not merely to celebrate a sacred ritual, but to recreate the atmosphere of the close bond shared in the Passover meal between Jesus and his disciples. The songs and readings fostered a feeling of deep affection, not only for God but for one another. It reached its crescendo in the breaking of the loaf of bread and the sharing of a single cup of wine that was passed from one to another.

One single loaf of bread, not little individual wafers, illustrating not separation but unity. Just as many kernels of wheat form one loaf, so many individuals form one body. One common cup, not little individual ones, poured out as a reminder that we are one people who share more in common than the differences that at times divide us. Many people in my previous parishes had insisted on separate communion cups so as not to risk getting sick from drinking after another person. It was a perspective which became more and more problematic for me personally, especially after living for three years in Papua New Guinea, where there were no such things as individual communion cups. The only communion cup option was any vessel that held liquid.

My pastoral exploits had also led me to Botswana, a country ravished by AIDS (referred to as the "skinny disease"), where communion was also celebrated with just one cup. I remember kneeling at a communion rail there and drinking after those dear souls, some of whom were obviously emaciated by this illness. I was overcome not by the fear of catching a disease, but by the profound sense of oneness I felt with the other members of the mystical body of Christ who were one with me. It was the same feeling of unity at Iona, where I was invited in worship to set aside all that separated me from others and instead focus on so much more that united us as God's beloved children.

This Agape service was much more than a required religious ritual in which one received bread and wine in whatever form for the real or imagined forgiveness of sins. This was a coming together as a community in the most holy and sacred sense of "communion," where all who were broken were united in the breaking of bread. In this breaking of bread, we joined with the One who suffered for us in the past and continues to suffer with us in the present. Communion also connected us to His body, which was present in everyone there. We shared this mystical experience of carrying one another's pain and suffering. We drank from the same cup containing not just wine but with a mystical Eucharistic elixir containing hope and healing. It was as if the hands that held the bread and wine during that first communion were being extended vicariously by means of the hands of each person there.

Oddly, I experienced a moment of spiritual dissonance and unrest during this divine meal. How different this was from my previous practice! It wasn't merely the fact that it was a woman leading this sacred rite, an anomaly in my Lutheran tradition, but the lack of rules and restrictions concerning who could or could not participate.

In my conservative Lutheran church, communion was closely controlled. Only members "in good standing" with us or another sister congregation were able to participate. An announcement in the bulletin clearly stated this policy with an attempt to justify it using theological rationale. If there was time before the service started, I would query the visitors about their church teachings and doctrinal beliefs and, based on their answers, would determine whether or not they were "worthy" to participate. Honestly, even as I write this, I shudder with shame as I reflect on the people I offended by zealously enforcing this practice. A loving God cannot be pleased with the pride that pervades a religious organization that restricts access to such a great gift, or the presumptuousness that takes up residence in the heart of a pastor who, in violation of his own conscience, enforces such a practice.

How different it was in the place I was now seated. Here, the only rule was love. The litmus test of one's worthiness was simply whether one hungered and thirsted to receive these life-giving gifts. The clergy person celebrating the service would remind those gathered that "The table is Christ's table and does not belong to any one church tradition." This practice turned the communion table upside down on my tradition. The barriers and boundaries around communion were broken, allowing anyone to participate. All were welcome. It wasn't a matter of getting God right, or even getting right with God at Iona. Rather, it was simply receiving the assurance that God was already more than all right with us.

At that first Agape, I had a choice to make: stick to the presumptuously proud and pietistic principals I'd been taught or break ranks in the interest of seeking a different kind of unity; a unity of brokenness, a unity found in the company of fellow seekers, a unity that created peace and joy and love. In the end, the choice was easy, and the spiritual dissonance I had briefly experienced dissipated; I eagerly received the bread and the cup, holding them in my hands and near my heart like one would a precious keepsake. The chains around my heart began to loosen in that service and would eventually fall off entirely.

Thursday was the Service of Commitment, the night before the guests would leave. In various ways, people were encouraged to take whatever they had experienced of God at Iona with them, not only to their homes but into the world. Following this service, we gathered for another communion of sorts at the local pub. It was both joyful and sad, as toasts were made to the friendships that had been formed and the bonding that had occurred during the previous week.

The Word of God was central to all these services. How softly that Word fell upon my ears as it was read by a variety of accents from Scottish to African and beyond. That Word went beyond what was spoken in the sanctuary or written in the Book, for it was a living word, vivified and exemplified in the lives of those who lived there. It was brought to life in the beautiful setting of nature, which engulfed the community. Sometimes, that Word came crashing in, demanding one's attention, but more often, it was spoken in the whisper of so many small and meaningful moments.

Though the services and the people leading them were all different, there was a striking similarity and common theme: "The Loving God is present and working in this place." The evidence of the Spirit moving in an unlimited and undefinable way was undeniable. As the Spirit moved into the world, it was simultaneously leading that world to Iona...and God.

Throughout my time there, I wondered about the marvelous mysteries of worship in this place. What a different style from what I'd been used to before, yet how familiar and comfortable it seemed. Like the repetitiveness of the waves, so too the worship at Iona had a pattern and rhythm. The Spirit of love and grace flowed into and through the people in this place and flowed out with the pilgrims as they left.

TWELVE

Loving Work

AS MUCH AS YOU HAVE DONE IT UNTO
THE LEAST OF THESE YOU HAVE DONE IT UNTO ME.
—Jesus of Nazareth

In the seventeenth century, a monk named Lawrence served in a Carmelite monastery in France. Formerly an uneducated soldier, Lawrence spent most of his time working in the kitchen. Rather than seeing it as demeaning or less than what he was capable of, Lawrence viewed it as an opportunity to connect with God in a very personal way. In his simple acts of cooking and cleaning he saw himself providing an invaluable act of service to God and others. To till the earth, tend the animals, or take responsibility for brewing the beer was, for Lawrence, an opportunity to participate fully and intimately with the Divine Life of Love. After his death, the lessons that he had learned were passed on to others through his writings, which he had kept secret. In time, these became the topic of a book entitled *The Practice of the Presence of God.*

The spirit of Lawrence lives on in the work at Iona. Work is an act of worship, an opportunity to practice the precepts of Jesus and humbly serve God by serving others. Work is not a means to an end, but an end unto itself. It is not a task to be performed out of obligation or with a paycheck as motivation, but as a special occasion, even a celebration. The work of Iona allows one to experience God differently. At Iona, the words of Jesus, "Whoever desires to be great among you must be least," are not pious platitudes but an integral part of the daily spiritual practice. Work at Iona isn't a burden, it is another form of worship.

A lot of work goes into keeping a large retreat center running; therefore, "Little Lawrences" are found everywhere at Iona. The work is performed primarily by three groups of people. First, by the paid staff who stay year-round, serving a maximum of three years. Though responsible for overseeing and managing the various departments, none are averse to rolling up their sleeves and working alongside others. Then there are the short-term guests. They are there for a retreat that is usually one week in duration. Part of the purpose of their time is to experience all aspects of life in a community. In that regard, they are expected to perform daily chores. Then there are the volunteers, of which I was one, whose tenure lasts anywhere from a few weeks to a few months. In exchange for the privilege of living at Iona and receiving free room and board and a small weekly stipend, the volunteers carry out four primary roles: cooking and kitchen clean-up, housekeeping, office and bookstore workers, and finally, general assistants. That was my role. If asked to describe what I did, I would respond, "A lot of everything and a little bit of nothing." Though I was quite busy, the work was neither too arduous nor demanding, but rather delightful and fulfilling. During my time at Iona, I never tired of the daily duties or repetitive tasks. Just the opposite, I found them exhilarating, renewing, and refreshing. There was personal freedom in the familiarity of the daily routine. This pattern promoted a type of unintentional contemplative practice. The ritual of sweeping and mopping a floor without thinking was quite therapeutic, allowing my mind, body, and spirit to wander elsewhere. Rooms with dirty floors, stained sinks, and grimy toilets became sacred receptacles where I could practice this form of prayer and a unique manner of meditation.

Following morning worship, the workday officially commenced. We passed through the cloisters and into the refectory where we received our daily work assignments. These included a wide variety of jobs including, but not limited to, cutting vegetables for soup, cleaning bathrooms, vacuuming hallways, sweeping stairways, dusting banisters, and mopping floors. At Iona I didn't need to long for my day off as I had done previously, as each day was a new opportunity to discover the joy and satisfaction hidden in each activity.

The work at Iona was so different for me, as it had nothing directly to do with the ministry as typically perceived, and yet it was ministry in a hidden form. It was not only humble service, but also, in its very nature, caused me to contemplate Christ. For example, in cleaning the bathrooms, there were two different colors of cleaning cloths. The pink was for the sink, and the blue was for the loo (the word for toilet in Scotland). Using them would lead me to consider the woman who mopped Jesus' brow or the towel that He used to wash the disciples' feet. This type of work was overlooked, underappreciated, or even looked down upon in the world that I had left. No compliments were rendered for an effectively washed dish, as there had been for a skillfully delivered sermon. And yet, there was so much more self-satisfaction in those overlooked and seemingly insignificant tasks. At the end of each day, I didn't feel empty and exhausted but refreshed and restored. On the surface, these chores weren't achievements; there would be no public recognition and little appreciation from others for performing them. They were important for their own sake. One worked not for a paycheck or promotion, not to be rewarded or admired, not to receive accolades, applause, or an occasional "Amen," but simply because there was work to do. Tasks like washing dishes, setting the tables, mopping floors, or cleaning the toilets were a reward in their own right. While performing those tasks, I found myself able to connect with God in a simple and intimate way, almost as closely as when I sat in the Abbey services. I felt the Presence of God more profoundly in a pile of dirty laundry than I had while preaching from the pulpit or publicly offering up prayers.

Fridays were the busiest day of the week, as they marked "changeover day." The guests from the previous week left on the morning ferry, and the next group shortly after noon on Saturday. We had one day to do a deep cleaning: change the beds, wash all the linens, mop and vacuum the floors, thoroughly clean the bathrooms from top to bottom, restock the supply closets, and finish cleaning and preparing everything necessary for the next group of forty or so guests to arrive.

On my first Friday, I was assigned housekeeping in the Abbey. The shift began with a brief meeting with the supervisor, Michelle. During ensuing conversations, I discovered that Michelle had been an executive in a company in the U.S. and needed a "life redirection." She left her high-powered and well-paying career and became part of the staff at Iona. Her story, though unique to her, was not unusual at Iona. I found I was in good company with those who had discovered that their lives were no longer serving them, God, or others well at all. We met with Michelle to review the list of duties, and then divided into three teams of two. My partner was Helen, a spiritual director from the Czech Republic. She had come to Iona in part to improve her English. Each of the approximately fifty beds required a clean bottom sheet, and then a fresh duvet cover. The bedrooms served as a learning lab, not only for how to do the duvets correctly, but also to learn about angels. Helen recounted stories about angels and their activities that she had witnessed in the lives of others, as well as in her own. "The difficulty we face, is not that there aren't angels, but that we simply fail to recognize them. My role is to help people do this, by introducing them to their own personal angel." This was a new territory to be treading.

"Patrick," she said, "Who is your angel?"

"I don't know," I replied. "I didn't know I had one."

"Everyone has an angel," she said. "Even if they're not aware of it. Perhaps it would help if you introduced yourself to your angel."

I had never heard of such a thing, and it struck me as strange and somewhat heretical.

"How do I do that?" I asked.

"It's quite simple. You find a quiet space, like Columba did, and invite your angel to meet you there."

"Okay," I replied, "I will try it for you."

"Don't do it for me; do it for you." She said, "You might be surprised at what happens."

I was somewhat skeptical, but after considering more carefully what she had said, I assured her that I would try my very best to do so. By the end of the workday, we had the beds stripped and remade and a good start on the laundry. But more importantly, I believe I had met one of God's angels in Helen. Her spirit and spiritual insights remained with me for the rest of my time at Iona.

It was common practice to wear aprons while working. When I put my apron on for work, I could feel myself change. Placing the apron over my head to prepare for my daily service was somewhat like placing stoles over my head to prepare for Sunday services. Stoles were originally meant to simulate the yoke placed on a beast of burden; for me, they were symbols of my own inflated opinion of myself, and what I imagined to be my spiritual status and significance in the eyes of God. When I put the stoles on, I should've felt like a servant, the way I felt when I put the apron on. But I didn't. When I wore them, I expected, and sometimes demanded respect, both for myself and for the "office" that I held. When I wore the clergy uniform, I believed it gave me authority over others. Over time, I was seduced into believing that I should be lauded for all my good pastoral works, paraded as loving acts done for God and others, but in truth, I had done it mostly to serve my insecure self. In time, I became the embodiment of the Pharisees, whom Jesus called whitewashed tombs, empty on the inside, trying to build their egos and fill their spiritual emptiness by being praised by other people.

That changed dramatically at Iona. With the help of the apron, I began to view myself more as a servant than a master. It provided a new context to envision the scene where Jesus wraps a towel around his waist and washes the disciples' feet. Jesus humbly served not only His disciples, but many others, some of whom were marginalized, living at the outer edges of society. During my years spent in pastoral ministry, I had at times attempted to emulate Jesus' servanthood. Unfortunately, I had never seen it for what it truly was: a lowering of oneself to lift another up; a time to engage with a loving God through a simple act of loving others. At Iona I learned on a visceral level, through the mere act of putting on an apron and getting to work, what it meant to be a servant.

Michelle was fond of telling guests at their orientation that while we were there to serve them, we weren't *their* servants. But in truth, I saw myself as such. For by serving them, I was serving God. And that made all the difference in the work that was done with and for others. At Iona

I began to see people not as parishioners, or as someone to proselytize, or even as colleagues and co-workers. I saw them as beloved people of God who were vessels of and containers for Christ, whether they recognized it or not.

Iona and the work I did there was transformational. Whereas I used to think of myself as a "somebody," I began to experience the joy of being a "nobody." I imagined myself returning to one of my former parishes and having a congregant come up and ask me excitedly, "What did you do on your pilgrimage at Iona?" I would've loved to see her reaction when I said, "I scraped dishes, scrubbed toilets, emptied the garbage, washed floors, and changed beds."

The daily duties were not all peaches and cream, and they did come with their own set of peculiar challenges. Nonetheless throughout my ten weeks on the island, I cannot recall a time when I dreaded going to work. I loved chopping vegetables and making home-made macaroni and cheese in the kitchen; I loved hanging up the laundry in the drying rooms, and then folding it later; I loved sweeping floors and mopping them; I especially loved preparing the fireplaces by carefully placing newspaper, then kindling, and then a few larger logs on top. My mother used to say that "Work is play, and play is work." I found that to be true at Iona, in large part because of the people I was working with.

First, of course, there was Abrahan from Paraguay. When I arrived, he worked in the Abbey kitchen, so I didn't see him very much. About halfway through my tenure, he switched to housekeeping at the MacLeod Center. This is where I spent most of my time, and from then on, the two of us spent a lot of time together. Abrahan had a wickedly clever sense of humor. He would invent ways to make the work more enjoyable, and sometimes annoy the head resident in the process. For example, when setting the tables Abrahan would attempt to make the cups and dishes on the tables color coordinated. Or he would mop the entrance in a way that would cover the entire floor and make navigating it safely somewhat hazardous.

Our friendship grew not only as we worked together, but also as we walked together. We would occasionally take long walks to lesser traveled places on the island, like the remote canyon near the marble quarry. There, sitting on the precipitous bank peering down at the waves crashing on the rocks, Abraham spoke about his home in Santa Maria de Fe Misiones, Paraguay. His ancestors were the Guarani people, depicted in the film *The Mission*.

"Much of what is depicted in the film is true," he said, "especially our love for music. I play the Paraguayan harp," he said. "And I love to sing. So does my mother."

He went on to recount his love for his mother, who had raised him alone and instilled in him a dedication to the Catholic Church along with his love for music.

"Mi mama encouraged me to come to Iona, even though she would miss me terribly. I knew I needed to come, but I hated leaving her."

That served as an introduction to the type of conversation that parents have with their grown children. In time our relationship would take on an almost father-and-son-like connection, with him calling me "Papi" and me referring to him as "Mijo." Like the marble in that quarry, our relationship became so solid that it remains intact to this day.

The MacLeod center was also the place where I made a lasting friendship with Britt. She was from Sweden, similar in age to me, and was also looking for redirection in life and reconnection with God. Due to some of her challenges with the English language, and my total ignorance of Swedish, we frequently found our attempts at communication quite entertaining. She referred to the language she communicated in as "Swenglish." Her room was in the MacLeod center, next to mine, so we shared the kitchen and lounge. Like me, she was an early morning riser, so we frequently shared "communion" over cornflakes and coffee. Many days we would find ourselves folding laundry in the drying room, which came to be called "Britt's Sauna." It was there that Britt told me about what it was like for her growing up as a pastor's daughter.

"My father enjoyed standing in front of people to preach, to sit on boards and groups both locally and nationally. He was a colorful leader who liked to express his opinion to people both inside and outside of the church. My sister, who is sixteen months older than me, had those same qualities and enjoyed the attention. I was never comfortable in that role.

I felt the expectations both from my father and the people in the church to be like him, or at least to act a certain way. I couldn't do it, even if I had wanted to." It helped me understand and better empathize with my own daughters who had also struggled with life in the church fishbowl.

Britt also was divorced, not only from her husband but from God, or at least from the church where she had first been taught of God. Although her father had been a pastor, or maybe because of it, she had left the church in her twenties and never returned. Because of her background, I found her to be very empathic, and trustworthy. A bit to my surprise I found myself opening to her, not only about ministry, but also about my marriage and other perceived life failures on my part. She helped me to reframe my perspective not only on the events but on myself. She had a very deep and intuitive perspective on the God who is not confined by church buildings or defined by religion. Britt introduced me to the God she had come to know outside the church. As I listened to her, I came to have an affinity for the God she knew, who seemed so much more forgiving, loving, and merciful than the God I had grown up learning about. Because of her experience and gentle nature, she would gently correct me when she thought I was being too critical of myself.

"You are too hard on yourself," she would remind me. "You must learn to be gracious and loving to yourself." The tone of her voice conveyed the kind of love she was encouraging me to receive.

There were others, too many to name, all of whom remain deeply embedded in my heart, and who became dear friends, as well as invaluable co-workers. And indeed, there was a great deal of work to be done at Iona; work that made it possible to encounter others in a Christ-like way. It was a different type of communion. When I worked alone, I could be still and contemplate. With the flurry of activities and the demands that filled a day, some found it difficult to find alone time. I didn't share that problem. And when I worked with others, I could be active and celebrate. Even amid the sometimes-chaotic work environment, even with the unusual physical demands placed on my body, I found that my soul was at peace, regardless of the surroundings. I also came to share an appreciation, understanding, and affinity for that ancient perspective on work that Lawrence, Columba, and so many of the ancient monastics had.

I met a loving God in the work I did at Iona and in the people I worked with. In the small, seemingly insignificant ways that I served, I was also served. At Iona, stooping down to wash the feet of others was not a ritual to be observed at an Ash Wednesday service once a year, but a daily reality in which one acknowledged the inherent worth of others.

Slowly, I began to recognize that value in myself. I was much less concerned about what people thought or said about me. I was in the process of cutting ties to my past and beginning to forge a new future. I wasn't becoming a different person but rediscovering who I'd always been. Perhaps for the first time since my teenage years, when I worked on the farm and in the cheese factory, I was fully present not only to what I was doing and why, but with and for Whom I was doing it.

THIRTEEN

Loving Presence

IN THE DEPTH OF WINTER, I FINALLY LEARNED
THAT WITHIN MYSELF THERE LAY AN INVINCIBLE SUMMER.
—Albert Camus, *Return to Tipasa*

L ife slows down at Iona. One day languorously gives way to another. In western culture, people are programmed to live either by eagerly antici- pating the next great event in the future or reliving the past. This doesn't translate to life at Iona. What matters most to the people there is living in the fierce urgency of now. The to-do lists that rule the worlds of people else- where are irrelevant. Rather than worrying about what needs done or what has been left undone, one finds freedom in welcoming whatever the day has in store. One discovers delight in the seemingly mundane daily events that would previously be avoided, overlooked, or ignored altogether. Even though there is a lot to do, one quickly discovers that there is more to being than merely doing.

The most meaningful moments at Iona are not so much sought after as stumbled upon, usually in the most unexpected places and people. The secret to experiencing such moments fully is to be fully present. Being present means being open spiritually and emotionally to welcome and receive whatever God might be communicating in the presence of others. Such moments can be experienced anywhere. They are not unique to Iona, but the slower pace, rhythm of daily life, and sacred nature of the place itself nurtures an environment where people are more attuned and better equipped to listen to what God is telling them. The lost art of listening is rediscovered at Iona, and I heard the still small voice of God spoken to me in the words of many of the men and women whose paths crossed mine. One memorable encounter was with Lisa, who invited me to sit with her on a small bench during an unusually sunny afternoon on the island.

I was aware of Lisa before I met her. Everett, another volunteer who had served as the assistant musician at Iona, played the organ at her church. He had pointed her out to me after one of the services and told me that I needed to meet her. He said that she was a great person, serving as a pastor in the Church of Scotland and shepherding a small congregation in Glasgow. For Everett, who was by his own admission a natural-born cynic and somewhat suspicious of people, this was quite a compliment. I was suspicious for other reasons.

In my tradition, women clergy were forbidden. It was a biblical mandate, we were taught, that due to the original sin of Eve as well as the prohibition by St. Paul, women weren't to hold authority over men. As such, women were not only denied ordination, but also the opportunity to hold other leadership positions. The ancient Celtic church had not taken such a patriarchal view of women and their service in the church. Historically, women were held in high regard, both in social and sacred settings. The Iona Community continued that tradition, warmly welcoming women clergy. Encounters with Lisa and others like her during my time at Iona would open my closed mind.

Lisa was a frequent visitor to the island. On this particular occasion, she was leading a group from her parish and community. Having completed my clean-up following the noon meal at the Abbey, I walked up the hill to my home at the MacLeod Center. It was a warm and sunny day, a rarity for Iona, even in the summertime. Lisa was sitting outside on a bench, soaking up the sunshine. Her calm and peaceful presence extended an open invitation to join her. I approached her and said, "You're Lisa, Everett's pastor, aren't you?

"Aye," she replied.

"Do you mind if I join you?"

"Not at all, please do," she said.

After exchanging initial pleasantries, we seamlessly settled into comfortable conversation which, like the tea in Scotland, flowed easily and abundantly.

"What brought you to Iona?" she asked.

I had grown weary of repeating my story to the many guests who rotated through the revolving door of Iona. At first, there was a therapeutic element in sharing a bit of my history, giving an elevator speech version of leaving ministry to come to this place. But I was careful about going into too much detail for fear of having to answer the difficult questions that would require full transparency and vulnerability. When I met Lisa, that changed. Though I was still a bit wary, I found a trusted confidant in Lisa. In her, I sensed a kindred spirit.

"I lost myself," I replied. "I lost me, and everything I held dear to me, including God and faith. I got tired of my life as a pastor. I no longer believed in what I was telling others to believe."

She didn't pry or try to fix whatever she thought might be wrong with me. Instead, she began to share about her own struggles in ministry.

"I can kind of understand," she said. "I've been in a similar place myself. Some years ago, I became the object of ridicule on the part of some of my parishioners, and the object of wrath on the part of a few. They criticized everything I said and did. I tried my best to make things right, to do what they expected. But it was never enough, so eventually I left."

She went on to tell of the betrayal she experienced at the hands of those she most trusted, the pettiness and mean-spiritedness in others, the desire for control and power on the part of leadership. Her story could've been mine, just set in Scotland instead of the U.S.

"I felt like I was fighting God's people for the sake of God's people," she said.

As I listened to her, I was struck with her empathy, honesty, humility, and vulnerability. And I realized I wasn't alone.

"I also walked away," she said. "And I came here to gather and renew myself. It took some time, but eventually, I was given a new opportunity to serve God and others. And I'm happy and fulfilled now."

Here was someone who understood! The brief telling of her story gave me permission to share mine. She sat listening attentively the entire time, not interrupting me, just allowing me to purge. And when I finished, she didn't stare at me incredulously, give me advice, or share over-utilized scripture passages, well-intentioned thought it may have been. Instead, she simply sat with me. And after a long time of silence, she asked the question, "Who are you?"

I knew that she wasn't inquiring about my heritage or background. She was interested in the *me* I had so carefully hidden within.

"I'm a beloved child of God," I answered.

I had learned this from reading Henri Nouwen, but by now, I was not simply mimicking his words; I had begun to truly believe and embrace them. I discovered that this new identity is not determined by what one does or has. It isn't defined by success or failure, nor dependent upon the opinion of others. When one recognizes that they are a beloved child, it is more than enough.

Lisa allowed time for another very long pause, perhaps pondering the veracity of my response or carefully considering her own, or maybe just allowing God to speak in the silence.

"Where are you most fully you?" she asked. I was caught off guard by this question.

"What do you mean?" I asked.

"Where is that place, and what are you doing there that allows you to be the person God intended you to be?"

For a guy who had prided himself on having all the answers, I was unable to respond. I stalled for time.

"I have no idea," I finally admitted.

I expected and perhaps hoped that she would provide her own insight or give me her opinion on what she thought. But she didn't. She didn't pursue her line of questioning. She didn't pry or try to lead me with some type of probing questions. She didn't pretend to know the mind of God or give me some expert advice based on her own life. In her gentle wisdom she knew that there was no "right" answer that she could give me. I had to discover that on my own. Her role was simply to ask the question, to create space. And listen.

In retrospect, I can clearly see that on that sunny afternoon on a bench at Iona, I met an Anam Cara, a Soul Friend. A Soul Friend is a person who, though you may never have met, you recognize immediately, as though you've known them all your life. A Soul Friend doesn't tell another person what they should do or how they should live. They don't try to give advice or talk someone out of their grief or depression. A Soul Friend comes alongside the other, as Jesus did with the disciples on the road to Emmaus, and accompanies them on their journey, if only for a short time, reminding them that they are not alone. What matters for an Anam Cara is to be fully present, to listen instead of speaking. And when the time does come to speak, it is not for the purpose of quoting a Bible passage as a proof text to whatever the person may be experiencing, nor is it to drum up a solution to a problem that isn't theirs, nor is it even to fill the sacred silence that seems so uncomfortable to those living in a culture filled with constant noise. What matters most is we recognize that we have been granted the privilege of standing on holy ground. There is nothing that we must *do*; it is only who we are called to *be* that matters. In those times we spend with an Anam Cara, we may very well be the closest we'll ever come to being in the Presence of God, at least this side of eternity. In the sacred other, we experience a living icon of God. This loving bond between two children of God is where we experience the indwelling of the Spirit, and the coexistence of the Divine.

That is a difficult idea for many of us to grasp, that in truth God resides within each person. This idea is counterintuitive to traditional church teachings. As the days of our lives accumulate, so do the errors, mishaps, and mistakes we make, or are deceived into believing that we have made. Unfortunately, rather than seeing those as simply being part of our common and collective human experience that may serve a transformative purpose, we instead consider them to be blights upon our being, an inaccurate reflection of what we are led to believe erroneously about ourselves: that we are horribly marred and misshapen humans unworthy of the love of

God or others, and therefore unable and unwilling to even love ourselves. Sometimes others become our willing accomplices in this case of mistaken identity, more than happy to heap on us the shame and guilt we are prone to in those times.

The Divine lives and moves within each person. Perhaps the most grievous sin is failing to recognize and reclaim our Divine life. Instead, we are too often inclined to focus on our faults and failures, our mistakes, and mishaps, which are a normal part of being human. Too many of us have been taught by the church that we are so horribly marred by human sin that we are unworthy of love. What a tragic, toxic, and untrue teaching, that each human being is something other or less than a receptacle for God's love. Too often this leads to feelings of guilt, shame, and hopelessness. At least that's where it led me. At Iona I was introduced to the God who is so far beyond any of that, and who intimately dwells within each person. In so doing God dispels those harmful human feelings and all that we feel makes us unworthy of love. It's a truth that St. Paul was aware of and bore witness to: "The mystery of godliness is great, which is Christ in you, the hope of glory,"[1] At Iona I came to not only appreciate, but to embrace this mystery more fully.

Iona was a daily reminder that we really are God's unique, one-of-a-kind creations. There never has, nor will there ever be, another living being exactly like us. God gave each one life by means of eternal respiration, filling us with the very breath of heaven, which is nothing other than the Spirit of God.[2] Jesus emphasizes this divine union and indwelling in the fourteenth chapter of the Gospel of John (the Celts' favorite Gospel, by the way). "I will pray to the Father, and He will give you another Comforter, the Spirit of Truth, who will abide with you forever ...who will dwell with you and will be in you...on that day you will know that I am in the Father is in me, and you in me and I in you."

Sometimes it seems that followers of Christ have focused on what the Holy Spirit can help them do for others or for God while conveniently forgetting what the Spirit has already done for us, namely delivering the

---

1 Colossians 1:27
2 The Hebrew word for spirit is *ruah*, which means "breath."

Divine to the very doorstep of our hearts. We are each a locus of the Divine Life that lives and moves and has her being within us. St. Paul said, "It is no longer I who live, but Christ who lives in me."[3]

This fundamental truth, believed and taught by the first followers of Christ, was either forgotten, lost, or locked away in the Western Church. Mainly this was a result of the confrontation that occurred between Pelagius, who was a Celt, and St. Augustine. Pelagius taught that the image of God was not completely lost in The Fall, and therefore mankind still retains some of that Divine goodness. Unfortunately, Pelagius lost that battle to St. Augustine who said that man is completely corrupted by sin from the very time of conception. This is the teaching that became normative in the Western Church and was embraced by everyone; everyone that is except the Celts who were far more influenced by Pelagius than by Augustine or the Pope. They continued to believe that the goodness of God was dwelling in and through all creation, which included human beings. John Philip Newell, renowned author on Celtic spirituality, put it this way:

> The infinite is consubstantiated with the human, so that what is most truly human is what is most divine. There is no part of our nature, as God made it and as God means it, that is not brought into the dearest nearness to Himself.[4]

Newell goes on to say that Celtic spirituality is "not looking away from life but more deeply into it … and that the life of our truest self partakes of the very substance of God's life, the Oneself that is at the heart of all Selves."[5] It was that momentary encounter with Lisa that made me begin to fully grasp this new insight.

After a long time sitting together, mostly in silence, Lisa got up and left, allowing me the grace and the space to consider what had just transpired. The exchange that we shared was something much greater than a good

---

3 Galatians 2:20
4 Philip J. Newel, *Listening to the Heartbeat of God: A Celtic Spirituality* (London: SPCK Publishing, 2008), 70
5 Newel, 70.

conversation; it was time spent in the Presence of God. The Spirit brought us together so that we might form a deep, divine connection, if only for a moment. Though we didn't know each other, our souls recognized one another as an Anam Cara.

Lisa opened me to a new and different way of thinking, not only about my life, about who I had been, but also about who I was becoming. I realized that despite all the changes experienced over the last several years, the one eternal constant was the deeply abiding presence and love of God. Experiencing the fullness of the Presence of God, like I had with Lisa, resulted not on arriving at life's answers, but living more fully into the questions.

There were many such revelations for me at Iona. At first, I saw the Divine in the place, then I perceived God in others, and finally I sensed God's presence working in me, especially as I shared those many magnificent moments, whether in conversation over a cup of coffee with a guest, taking spontaneous walks with a stranger, engaging in unexpected and unscheduled activities with other volunteers or staff members, or simply sitting silently with another person or by myself. I came to see that these blissful and heavenly moments were reciprocal, made not merely by the Spirit of God working through others for my sake, but in and through me for theirs as well.

Perhaps most importantly, my time at Iona allowed me to see the past drifting away, being washed out to sea, and no longer being of any consequence. And rather than anxiously peering into the future with worry and anxiety, I began anticipating instead the unexpected awe that comes from encountering God. It was that type of wonder-full experience, not happiness, that I began to desire and seek. Iona introduced me, as well as others, to God's Loving Presence. Greta, a volunteer from Germany, was one of those people.

Following one of the Friday morning farewells, Greta and I walked together on the back path to the Abbey. As we passed through the green pasture that gently sloped down toward the sound on our right, with the Abbey looming up ahead, she softly said, "My soul is at home here."

"Why?" I asked her. "What is it about this place that makes it so special for you?"

She couldn't fully express herself, not because English was her second language, but because there are some spiritual truths that are impossible to put into words. We walked the rest of the way to the Abbey in silence.

I can only surmise that part of the reason Greta's soul was at home at Iona was due to the all-permeating Presence of God. The ancient sacred elements of the souls that comprise the character of the place push their way from the past into the present. Iona is a place steeped in history, and is unique geologically, different even from the mainland from which it is separated by little more than a stone's throw. If one is carefully looking and listening, the Presence of God can be encountered frequently. Here, God is ever-present, welcoming all those who come seeking God, and when they discover God, they also find themselves and their true home. Perhaps that is the real reason Columba stayed here; he had come home. Perhaps that is the reason Greta's soul was at home at Iona. I am certain that I sensed it frequently at Iona and have been more aware since I left.

"Where are you most fully you?" In the years since leaving Iona, I have been on a quest to answer that question. My journeys have taken me many places, but finally I believe I have arrived at an answer: "Wherever I am fully present in the moment with Another, that is where I am fully me, and where God is present with me." It is the Loving Presence of God that I experienced with Lisa as the three of us sat together on that sunny afternoon.

FOURTEEN

Loving Creation

THE LAND SPOKE LIKE A TEMPLE,
THE RIVER'S JOURNEY WAS WINDING.
TO THEIR KNEES THE VALLEYS GENUFLECTED
THE SIGN OF THE CROSS ON THE BRANCHES.
I HEARD THE GOSPEL ON THE WIND
AND HOLINESS WAS UPON THE EARTH.
THIS WAS WHERE MY FIRST LOVE LIVED
I'D NOT BEEN THIS WAY FOR SO LONG.
—Sean O'Riordan *The Pilgrim's Song*

In the ninth century, a Celtic theologian named John Scotus Eriugena[1] fled the Viking raids in Ireland, leaving his monastic life to take up residence in the court of Charlemagne. While serving as the emperor's chief theologian, Eriugena developed the teaching now called "panentheism." Distinct from pantheism, which is the belief that everything *is* the very nature of God, panentheism recognizes that while everything that is comes *from* God and that God is in everything, the divine nature of God transcends all of this. This teaching summarizes the Celtic perspective on creation and humanity which admires and adores this world as a place that not only mirrors the sacred but contains the sacred as well.

---

1 Scotus was a common name for someone who was Celtic, and Erigena meant "from Ireland."

The ancient Celts recognized, relished, and revered their connection with God in creation. They had a fully formed natural knowledge of God; it was reflected in their daily life of work, prayer, and praise. All the elements essential for a healthy spirituality flowed together. The Celtic shape of the cross itself, with the circle forming a holy halo around the cross-arms, reflected this concept. They didn't distinguish, as Western Christianity did, between the secular and the sacred. They did not neatly divide the domain of God within the church versus the realm of the everyday outside of it. Everything belonged to God, everything and everyone was sacred. God was, and is, present in, with, and under all things. This is clearly captured in the Lorica of St. Patrick:

> I arise today through a mighty strength, the invocation of the Trinity,
> Through a belief in the Threeness, Through confession of the Oneness,
> Of the Creator of creation.
> I arise today through the strength of heaven.
> Light of the sun, Splendor of fire, Speed of lightning,
> Swiftness of the wind, Depth of the sea, Stability of the earth,
> Firmness of the rock.

In his book *Beauty*, Irish author and poet John O'Donahue expands upon and elucidates the view of the Celts described by Eriugena and Patrick. He invites the reader to encounter God in the beauty of creation for the purpose of simple appreciation and soul restoration. "The human soul is hungry for beauty," O'Donahue writes. At Iona, it's as if the beauty O'Donahue describes in the book springs to life, leaping off the pages and providing a living illustration in the environs of the island.

The beauty of God greets each day in both subtle and obvious ways. Beauty is experienced as one walks along the beach, eyes treated to the changing colors of the sea, at times turquoise, at others a midnight blue, and still others a deep, dark black. One can feel the beauty penetrating the soul as the waves rhythmically make their march toward land, in some places crashing violently on the rocks and in others slapping softly upon the sodden sand. Beauty is seen in the adorable forms of the Highland cattle, or *Heilan coo*; contentedly grazing, as well as in the unique cry of the Corn Crake.[2] Beauty is felt in the smooth stones at St. Columba's Bay and is easily detected as one walks through the quaint village, and along the quiet seaside quay. Beauty abounds at Iona. It is as if one is stepping onto the easel and into the scene which the Artist is painting, becoming a living participant of the masterpiece. But what makes the beauty of Iona unique from other places is not only perceiving God in the beauty of the place, but feeling the actual embrace. It is as if one is being wrapped up completely in the essence of God's Spirit.

Before arriving at Iona, the brilliant colors of life's beauty had faded into gray for me. I was numb to the eternal exhilaration, unable to appreciate the divine footprint found in creation. It was as if cataracts were covering my eyes. My heart and soul were drifting through life like wayward wanderers through a pall of cloudy smoke. My view of God was obfuscated, my perspective narrowed to a pinpoint. I was suffering from religious tunnel vision, experiencing spiritually what some people with dementia experience physically: a loss of peripheral vision and an inability to see anything that is not immediately in front of you. This dark and distant view of God had resulted in the spiritual dehydration of my soul, which had become dried up and withered, desperately needing to be watered and brought back to life. It had been a slow and insidious process that I now realize began in a place one would never imagine such a process occurring: the seminary.

In Western theology, Christians are wont to confine the divine by limiting God to their cognition. Seminary codified this practice for me; I limited my knowledge of God to doctrines and dogmas, tractates, and treatises, in order to know everything possible about God—and get good grades, of course. I didn't recognize it at the time, but there is a difference between knowing *about* God and *knowing* God. The more I learned in terms of head knowledge, the further it led me from experiencing God with my heart, the place I had first met God. Nonetheless, the purpose of my pastoral training was to know everything I could about God, so that I might convey that information to others. However, my religious training failed to teach

2 A small brown bird found only in this part of the world, making Iona a popular destination for another group of people: Bird Watchers.

me how to personally experience God in a more meaningful way. Slowly, my heart calcified, becoming like petrified wood that protected me from the hurts that ministry naturally imposed. God was not close and compassionate, but distant, cold, and for the most part uncaring. To the extent that God was alive for me, it was in the dead letter of God's ancient law. Like an anchorite, God was sequestered to a very small space, with the holy scriptures as the only window through which I could peer in. There, God was securely kept at a safe distance. I never learned how to appreciate a God who can be known in ways outside of an objectively strict and rigid interpretation of scripture, such as creation.

It is certain that children, having just come from God, are born with a natural knowledge of the Divine. They have an intuition that allows them to be in tune with God, which few of us retain as we age. I was no exception. I was born and raised surrounded by the wild outdoors of northern Wisconsin. My faith was fashioned by the woods and water and wildlife. I sensed that each tree adorned with green in the summer, wearing a laurel of orange and red in the autumn, and stripped bare by the bitter cold in winter reflected the glory of God. When I stepped outside of my door and experienced nature firsthand, I believed I was in the Eden I'd read about in my children's Bible. My imagination ran free in the woods across the dirt road in front of my house. I built tree houses that transported me back in time to the days when the mountain men and pioneers built their log cabins and simple sod dwellings. I watched in wonder as my dad tapped maple trees and boiled down the sweet sap to make maple syrup. I stood transfixed as Dad taught me my first lessons on how to safely use a shotgun or rifle. At times I became Daniel Boone or Davy Crocket as I hunted squirrels and rabbits with my 410-gauge shotgun in the big woods behind my house. On more than one occasion I had the bejeebers scared out of me when a partridge took flight, testing my instinctive reflexes to track and pull the trigger in time, before it flew away.

I experienced the pleasures of a land wet and wild and teeming with heavenly wonders, full of flora and fauna, all beckoning me to join the adventure. I also experienced the unpleasantness the land had to offer, nettles and poison ivy, mosquitos and wood ticks, scrapes and bumps, and the occasional broken bone. These were the natural consequences that came as the result of being too careless. But it wasn't punitive on creation's part, but just the natural order of things. Long before ever being formally catechized, I learned of life and death from the small farm I lived on, and in the realm of the wild world that surrounded me. Life was vibrant, precious, sometimes short, and always unpredictable. But there was also the constant reminder that the natural rhythm of life involved not only death, but restoration, renewal, and resurrection.

Through God's creation, I witnessed the beauty of Eden in the wilderness, like the whitetail deer gracing the fields and forests. I also witnessed the brutality of Eden's fall when those same white tail deer fell dead from a gunshot, their lifeblood flowing from them, and staining the snow crimson. It was in this wild kingdom that I spent time with my earthly father, and my Heavenly Father as well. My father's pleasure came from practical things necessary for survival, like farming, gardening, and hunting. As a result, most of my quality time with my father revolved around spending time outside. That's where we bonded. I'd get home from school, and we'd take a walk in the woods, with our guns of course. In his own way, my father taught me about life, death, and the necessity of taking another life to survive in a sometimes cruel and unforgiving world. The outdoors was father's sanctuary, though he did agree, mainly out of obligation to my mother, to occasionally visit the sanctuary constructed by human hands. What I discovered, to my dismay, is that the lessons learned in man's church sometimes contradicted those taught in God's.

Every Sunday service began with the invocation, "I believe in God the Father Almighty, maker of heaven and earth." In my heart, I believed what my mouth was saying, for this is what I was living daily. But even then, a question crept into my mind: *Why did creation have to be so closely tied to only a Father, and not a Mother as well?* After all, that's how nature worked. Up until then, I had witnessed women feeding and providing for people all the time, which seemed quite consistent within the context of the creation which provided our sustenance. The lesson from the fauna, the farm, and the flood of Noah is that God created both male and female, and both were necessary. The emphasis on only a male God that I got in church and

Sunday school seemed strangely inconsistent with the evidence I saw all around me.

The confession of sins followed the invocation. In it, we were required to come clean with sin, in a very common kind of way. There was no laundry list of bad words and actions that had to be verbalized like my Catholic friends described in their confession. Instead, everyone just joined together in admitting that, basically, we were rotten human beings. We weren't really to blame for this; it was the fault of Adam and Eve, who, when they disobeyed God's explicit orders not to eat the forbidden fruit, plunged the world into sin and, as a result, got themselves expelled from the Garden of Eden. Even then, as a young boy, I felt this was all a bit unreasonable. *If God didn't want them eating from that tree, why did He put it there in the first place?* The punishment certainly didn't seem to fit the crime: eternal death and damnation for eating an apple, or whatever the forbidden fruit was? I compared it to the punishments that I occasionally received from my parents and found the God of Genesis to be unreasonable, unpredictable, and apparently far too fond of punishing people.

In addition to learning about a capricious God, the church taught that the world, though it was once good, had become bad. Really bad. So bad, in fact, that it forced God to step away. And so, God created a space called heaven that was safer, more satisfying, and suitable for the Holy One's habitation. Meanwhile, we human beings were stuck on earth, which was now completely corrupted by all forms of sin imaginable, not at all like it was intended to be. Like Adam and Eve, we had been banished from the garden, and the earth we now inhabited was evil, and so were we. It was all so wicked, in fact, that God wanted little to do with it. The plan was to eventually destroy it. This God was biding his time until he could wreck it all in a terrifying way and then rebuild it. It was as if creation itself had gotten the better of God, and so now God had become a religious recluse, taking refuge in a more secure and sacred place, the church.

The implication was that God preferred the church building, evidently because it wasn't nearly as dirty, despicable, or dangerous as the great outdoors and thus far more worthy as a holy habitation. God had been moved into a secure neighborhood, a gated community, so to speak. The institutionalized and organized church was God's new home. This home was sacred *and* sanitary. Here in the church, things were clean, neat, and tidy. It wasn't just the people populating the pews, all decked out in their Sunday best, not just the pastor parading around the sanctuary in vestments designed to convey virtue, giving the impression of being wholly or holy sanctified, but also the kitchen and the lawn and the flower beds and the stained-glass windows and everything in and with and under this dominion. Even to a young boy, it seemed to be far too sterile, insincere, and phony, conveying the unspoken message that if the church building wasn't kept up properly, God just might leave and go live with the Catholics.

It was all so unbecoming and unreasonable. Even as a child I was suspicious. Why would God create everything and call it good, and then change his or her mind and decide to abandon it all? For me, it was a hell of a lot more fun spending time outside in nature than within the sterile confines of a building, sitting through unbearably long, boring services. My impression of this man-made sacred space was that it was populated by some very unpleasant-looking and acting people who were led by a clergyman whose main joy seemed to be in telling us how displeased God was with us.[3] And sometimes, if the pastor got wind that someone in the congregation or community had been especially ill-behaved, we'd be threatened with the hell and damnation that was certain to be visited upon us.

Eventually I was forced to surrender to this religious propaganda. Seventh grade marked the start of my formal religious instruction. I spent two years preparing for my confirmation, the Christian version of a bar or bat mitzvah. If I didn't make my confirmation, my mother would be heartbroken and my dad mad as hell. In the interest of pleasing my parents, my pastor, and my God, I gave in. I believed what I was told, but secretly still rejected the patently absurd idea that God was to be found in one place to the exclusion of another. I could still enjoy the outdoors, but not as the domain of the Divine, at least not properly speaking. I did enjoy the weekly

---

3 In time I learned that Lutherans called this the Law, and it was intended to provide balance to the Good News that God loves us and forgives us our sins. I received a full portion of the fist, but somehow missed out on most of the second part.

lessons with the new pastor, fresh out of the seminary. He was much less intimidating than the old guy he replaced. The decision to eventually study for the ministry came more as the result of admiring him and desiring to please my parents than it did my own motivation to be a minister.

The years in seminary and pastoral ministry provided a more formal training in the ways that God works. What began as education became indoctrination, as I came to accept, and even defend, the conservative teachings of the organized church.

At Iona I was reminded of what, and whom, I had long since forgotten. I again heard the familiar voice of my Father. It was a voice calling in the wilderness. Not an angry voice, like I imagine John the Baptist used, but a still, small voice like the one that whispered to Elijah. I heard the whisper in the morning mist. I heard the whisper in the winds that would whip off the Atlantic. I heard the whisper in the rain that one minute was falling softly on the path, and the next pelting the windowpanes. I heard God's voice in the kind words of others. Iona opened the eyes and ears of my heart, long-since closed. And I listened. For the first time in years, I was not concerned with what I had to say to others about God but what God had to say to me. Iona reminded me that God cannot be confined to one space, one sacred place, one denomination or religious organization, or within the narrow confines of a book or building. At Iona, God showed me what I once knew but had forgotten; "I am still found in the places where you first found me." Being in creation allowed me to be with God again. Though far away from where I grew up, I felt like I was home again.

But why was I surprised? Others had tried to tell me! Creation was, as St. Francis said, God's first Bible. In the Bible, creation was the first place God chose to dwell, and it was the place where God often appeared to His people. In fact, God led them both into and out of the wilderness. God used the wilderness to speak. The prophets made it a primary residence. The monks of old left the populated places to find God in the deserted places. And Jesus Himself spent long periods of time in creation, experiencing the presence of the devil as well as God in the wilderness. In a sense, Iona became my own wilderness experience, my journey to a faraway place to rediscover God in the place God had always been found; creation. I heard the voice of God not only speaking again in creation but singing as well. God desires to have His creation join together in a grand symphony of praise. I became part of that symphony one day amid the ruins of the Nunnery.

Because the weather was warm and sunny, an uncommon occurrence in Scotland, I decided to skip my short nap and take a walk by myself. As I approached the ruins of the Nunnery, I noticed a few delicate flowers blooming along one of the interior walls. I sat down, closed my eyes, and listened. I attempted to sense with my heart what was happening around me and in me. After a short time, I opened my eyes and watched the choreography of creation, designed by the Divine, as birds flitted to and from on the small wall, bees busily buzzing on and off the buds and flora extending outstretched tendrils to receive, relish, and rejoice in the radiance of the sun. Occasionally, a tourist wandered through, oblivious to what they were missing, and broke the spell. I felt sorry for them and their haste. I had done the same for so much of life, running from one thing to the next, preoccupied with matters that seemed important at the time. I had confused busyness with meaningfulness. Here in this garden, I was reminded that celebrating creation is a participation in the life of God.

Every week the Iona Community designated one of the evening services to God's presence in creation. One memorable night, Mark, a volunteer, led one of those services. He told the story of being at a birthday party for a friend's child. Having opened the gifts, the child began playing with his favorite toy. Somehow, the toy broke. The child took the toy to his parents, who told him that they would buy him a new toy to replace that one. Through his tears, he said, "I don't want a new one. I want this one fixed." Certainly, Mark said, that must be how God sees this world. We've broken it. Well-intentioned Christians unwittingly and carelessly contribute to the breaking of creation while waiting for a new one. But perhaps God does not desire that, but rather that we work together on fixing this one. We may not be able to repair it, but we can each do our part to responsibly care for it, like we would a sick friend or relative.

As I left the Abbey that night I continued to listen, to pray, to speak to my long since forgotten Friend. I believe the prayer went something like this:

> There is no plant in the ground, but tells of your beauty,
>> O Christ; There is no creature on the earth, there is no life
>> in the sea, but proclaims your goodness.
> There is no bird on the wing, there is no star in the sky, there is
>> nothing beneath the sun, but it is full of Your blessing.
> Lighten my understanding of Your presence, all around,
>> O Christ;
> Kindle my will to be caring for creation.
>
> —Celtic Prayers from Iona

FIFTEEN

Loving Pilgrimage

LOVING GOD IS A LIFELONG PILGRIMAGE, A LABYRINTH
WALK THAT IN THIS MORTAL LIFE NEVER FULLY REACHES THE
CENTER POINT. THE OBJECT OF OUR DESIRE WANTS US EVEN
MORE THAN WE WANT THE DESIRED ONE. IT IS GOD WITHIN
US THAT ALLOWS US TO FALL IN LOVE WITH GOD.
—Kenneth McIntosh, *Water from an Ancient Well*

Peregrini is the name Celtic Christians used for a pilgrimage. It is what St. Columba did when he made the short journey from his home in Ireland to Iona. But at the time it was akin to moving to another country, another world even. Leaving one's home and traveling to an unknown place was considered a "white martyrdom" by the Celts. Red martyrdom meant one died for the faith. White symbolized the purifying nature of a person's departure from family to permanently live elsewhere. It was martyrdom in the very real sense that the person was putting to death her former life. There would be no coming back if she changed her mind. It involved, especially for women, the very distinct possibility of it being a real, physical death.

Pilgrimage is part of the DNA of Iona. Since Columba first set foot on the tiny island, others have followed his lead. Iona became a destination for those seeking solace, safety, and, most importantly, the sacred. Today, Iona serves as a beacon for weary life wanderers seeking refuge from an unwelcoming, unforgiving, unloving, and unsafe world.

Honoring the spirit of Peregrini, mini-pilgrimages are held on the island every Tuesday. A pilgrimage that starts at the Abbey and goes the short distance to the Nunnery is offered for those whose mobility may be limited. The other option is a pilgrimage of approximately seven miles that consumes most of the day. Only the residential staff trained in first aid and safety can serve as pilgrimage guides. Due to my work schedule, I had only one opportunity to go on the pilgrimage. Henry, the Abbey musician, led our group. Some of the sites had become familiar from my previous personal excursions, but as Henry detailed each site with in-depth descriptions, I appreciated their significance even more.

We began our trek outside of the Abbey church, at the base of Columba's hill and at the foot of St. Martin's Cross.[1] Even though the Abbey dwarfs it, the cross still looms large over the surrounding landscape. It is a relic of times past, a reminder of the "high crosses" which were popular and prominent in the practice of the Celtic Christian faith. These crosses were placed outside in open areas to provide a gathering place to worship in the expanse of God's creation. It also honors the man whom it is named after.

St. Martin, better known as Martin of Tours, was a Roman soldier in the fourth century. His conversion to the Christian faith came about as the result of his encounter with a beggar. The man was freezing and asked Martin for a blanket. Martin didn't have one, so he took his knife, cut his cloak in half, and gave one-half to the man. That night, in a dream the identity of the beggar was revealed to Martin: Jesus. The words of Jesus, "As much as you have done it to the least of these my brethren you have done it unto Me," cut Martin to the heart and he experienced an immediate conversion. He left the military to devote the rest of his life to serving Christ and the poor. His cross is a memorial to the calling that each follower of Christ has to do likewise. It is also a symbol of the commitment of the Iona Community to serve those who suffer throughout the world.

As humans, we all suffer at times. Our suffering is unique to each of us and affects us in uniquely painful ways. During my years of ministry, I had many opportunities to be with people who were suffering, and to some

---

1 For a description of the pilgrimage, I draw not only on my own experience, but also on that given in the Iona Abbey Worship Book.

extent vicariously experiencing suffering with them: the grief over the loved one now gone, be it due to death or desertion; the fear and resentment over being fired from one's job and the ensuing financial loss; the slow and debilitating descent into helplessness from aging, arthritis, Alzheimer's and other agonies of body and mind; or the arrival at that place in life where dreams haven't materialized or no longer really matter. We all must carry a cross in some shape or form, a burden that at times seems too much to bear. It is the cross of St. Martin; the cross of Christ; the cross of the beggars. The heavy burden we bear is why some seek the succor that a spiritual pilgrimage can bring.

Taking leave of St. Martin's Cross, our small band of pilgrims meandered down the single lane road, walking a path trod many times before. The nunnery ruins, located within a stone's throw of the small village, was the next stop. This was the dwelling place of women who left everything and became pilgrims themselves, traveling to this isolated island. They did so to devote their lives to God and the church. It is a church whose history holds the heavy burden of having maligned, mistreated, and even murdered some of them. We stood in solemnity as we listened to the story of those who faithfully lived and died in loving service to God and others. Henry invited us to speak out loud the names of those women who had been important in our own lives. "Jean," my mother, immediately came to mind. This was followed in rapid succession by "Katie, Kayleen, Meghan, and Molley," my daughters. Those were the easy ones. Next came my sisters, "Linda, Mary Jo, Susie, Leeann." The Spirit led me to breathe a request for forgiveness and peace to surround each of them for the hurt that continued to linger years after the death of my mother. The last name I spoke was the most difficult, that of my ex-wife, Pam. As I said her name, I uttered a prayer for healing from all the hurts I inflicted upon her during our years of marriage, and the pain I still felt for the severing of our sacred bond. My momentary melancholy was interrupted by Henry's soft, melodic singing, providing a subtle invitation to conclude our prayers and take leave of the ruins. As we did, I sensed the call to also move on from the ruins in my life and the damage I'd caused in the lives of others, leaving them firmly rooted in the past.

Our next stop was at the crossroads. It is the only four-way intersection on the island. I looked at our cohort and realized how appropriate this stop is. Many of us had come to this place disoriented and in need of direction, unsure of what road to follow. For some of us, the road we had been traveling on for so many years had become a dead end. Now we were looking for a new road to walk. Perhaps a few of us would find that new path during our time at Iona. For some it would provide renewed strength sufficient to continue our journeys. There were occasional conversations as we left the crossroads, but for many, me included, we preferred quiet contemplation. I desired to use this time to consider the paths that had brought me to that place, and to enjoy each of the moments that comprised this unique time and space.

Next we arrived at the "Christmas Tree." At the time of Columba, the island would have resembled a forest, but this lonely evergreen was the only remaining tree on the island. As I stood listening to Henry, I found myself experiencing something that might be described as an Ebeneezer Scrooge moment, for it was as if I were visited by the ghost of Christmas past.

My most recent Christmas was the first to pass by. It was the last Christmas season spent in pastoral ministry and in my old house. What a drastic difference between the warmth I felt in my old farmhouse, stockings hung from the mantle over the fireplace, well-lit and decorated Christmas tree glittering in the corner in front of the bay way window, potpourri putting out a pleasing aroma, surrounded by my family, and the coldness that crept into my heart as I did my best to celebrate in the house of God with the congregation. Quickly that discomfort was dispelled by the Christmas prior to that one, which was engulfed by the joyful arrival of my first grandchild, born only four days earlier. That precious grandson, my first, was the best Christmas gift imaginable.

That memory was replaced by Christmas, 2010, the year of my divorce. Through my cloudy memory, I see three things clearly: Sharing my daughters with Pam on Christmas Day, the gaping hole in my heart, and drinking too much after everyone left. I recalled the discomfort and pain of the occasion, trying to keep things the same but knowing that from that point forward in our family, holidays would never be the same. Quickly, I hurriedly pushed that memory away and searched for another to take its place; I landed on the last Christmas I celebrated with my mom. I wondered if, even then, she knew who I was or where she was. I chased that one away and chose instead to think of the three Christmases I experienced in Papua New Guinea, when my girls were young, and the celebration was much simpler. Then there is the Christmas before I was married, when my then fiancée attended *The Nutcracker* in Chicago. It seemed then that the magic on stage reflected the magic that would be present in our marriage.

Finally, my thoughts traveled back forty-eight years to my favorite Christmas as a child, the one when Santa surprised me with the gift of a puppy. It was Christmas Eve, and suddenly, my parents informed me that Santa was at the door. Cradled in his arms was a small, lively, black ball of fur. It was my very own dog. Buddy and I quickly became best friends. We had wonderful days roaming the woods together. Those days stretched out for eight glorious years, but at the age of twelve, my dad returned home one morning shortly after leaving for work to inform me that Buddy had been hit by a car and was dead. I would need to get him and bury him.

The half-mile walk I made down that dirt road in front of my house was one of the longest I've taken in my life. From a distance I could see his lifeless form, a crushed bundle of fur and bones. I gently picked him up and cradled him in my arms. Carrying him back to the house, I grabbed a shovel out of the garage, and then headed toward the woods where we had spent so much time together. Finding what I felt was the perfect resting place, I slowly dug a shallow grave where I placed his soft, lifeless form. Performing my own version of a funeral, in imitation of others I had attended, I eulogized Buddy, and thanked God for the best of Christmas gifts.

The following Sunday, still grieving the death of Buddy, I asked my Sunday school teacher, Mrs. Ewing, if Buddy would be in heaven. The lesson she taught may have been more valuable and comforting than any I would receive in all the years of my later training. "Ralphie, God wants us to be happy in heaven. Would it make you happy to have Buddy there?" she asked.

"Yes," I answered.

"Then I'm sure he has gone to heaven."

I can still see the red hair framing the face of Mrs. Ewing in what appeared to be the angelic face of the most beautiful woman, other than my mother, I had ever known.

The ghost of Christmas past took leave of me as I was beckoned back to the present. The sudden sound of singing by the group awoke me from my dream-like stupor. It was a Christmas hymn, "O Tannenbaum," being sung in a variety of languages representing the country of origin of each of the Iona pilgrims.

Our next stop was the Marble Quarry. Iona marble is like none other in the world. It is white with large veins of dark and light green running through it. In ancient times it was believed to have healing powers. Pilgrims collected small pieces of the marble to serve as talismens, and children from the seventeenth century on would sell them. The altar and baptismal font in the Abbey are made of Iona marble. The quarry as a business enterprise was short-lived. An old piece of rusty machinery remains, a relic that reminds us that all that humankind creates will eventually come to ruin.

Crossing over a large outcropping of rock, we moved down a hill, steep by Iona standards, and toward St. Columba's Bay. Columba and his disciples purportedly first disembarked from their small coracle here on Pentecost Sunday, 563. Legend has it that Columba climbed a hill and looked back to see if Ireland was still visible. It wasn't, so he decided to stay.

I sat on a sheltered crag of rocks with the waves dancing around them. Salty sea air occasionally hit me in the face as I ate my sack lunch—a sandwich, apple, and bag of crisps (potato chips). "What was it like for them," I wondered, "to leave everything they knew, knowing they'd never return?" I considered what I had left to come to this place, and what I would have to leave here when I departed.

After lunch, the group gathered around Henry to receive instructions about a ritual we were invited to perform.

"Take time to choose two stones," Henry said. "The first will symbolize the load that you have carried to Iona. It can include anything you have experienced in your past that has weighed you down. Place upon this stone all the hurts and heartaches that have caused you pain, and that you still carry with you today. When you have finished, take that stone, and throw it as far as you can into the sea. Then take the other stone and use it to symbolize the freedom you have from the past. It will serve as a memorial of your time today, and the life that you are taking with you when you leave Iona." Quickly we all went our separate ways, seeking just the right rocks.

I found my first stone quite quickly, a slightly red-colored rock about the size of my fist. I placed my hand on the rock. With that gesture, I tried to transfer all the negative energy associated with my past problems and the people and events that I deemed at least partially responsible for having caused them. I heaved the rock as far as I could into the surf. Briefly, I wondered what would happen if someone unwittingly stumbled upon that very stone loaded down with my troubles and kept it. Would they be the unknowing and unfortunate recipients of my own misfortunes? Would the stone have dark powers, parlaying to them in some form my own personal problems? Quickly dispelling these thoughts, I began the search for another rock, this one a "keeper." I wanted it to be just right. I moved to a place where fewer people were searching. I came across a stone that looked to me like it had a cross on it. Perfect. Picking it up and placing it into my pocket, I was determined to keep it forever as a permanent reminder of the new life I was embarking on.

That lasted only a few hours, as later that day, I met again with Britt.

"I went to St. Columba's Bay on the pilgrimage today," I said.

"Oh, I wish I could've gone one last time. How was it?" she asked.

"It was so incredible. The most meaningful part for me was the ritual on the beach." I explained it to her and showed her the stone with the cross. As I did so, it occurred to me that our journeys were very similar, and that she needed that stone as much as I did.

"Here, I would like you to have this. As a reminder of your journey."

"Thank you, dear brother," she replied, as tears of joy rolled down her cheeks.

In future times I would wish for that stone. But it taught me an unintended lesson: the burdens we carry can be so much lighter if we share them with others.

As I slowly made my way back to the group I overheard one member questioning Henry about the practice, as in her opinion it is preferable to leave the stones unturned and untouched. That's the desire we have for our lives, to be left alone and at peace. But life doesn't work like that. Nothing and no one are allowed to remain in a natural, peaceful, condition. There is always something or someone that dislodges life as we know it and carries us to a place we could not have imagined and never wanted to go. While the two of them discussed the matter of removing the stones, the rest of us became treasure hunters, combing the beach for other keepsakes.

After a brief tea break at the far end of the Machair, where we took time to review the morning we'd spent together, we moved on to the hermit's cell. All that remains of the hermit's cell is a small ring of rocks. I could only wonder why monks who were already living in seclusion needed another place to isolate themselves even further. Extroverts would not have done well. Standing amid these stones, I thought of my own isolation and how lonely I had been. I felt isolated when I was by myself, and when I was surrounded by others as well. Sundays were especially difficult as I no longer had my wife and children in church with me and had to return to the stifling silence in my house, my own hermit's cell of sorts.

But as I reflected on those five years, it occurred to me that I had not been alone, just as those hermits hadn't been. Though I wasn't aware of it, the Spirit that was present with them had also been with me. And it dawned on me that those who had secluded themselves were not doing so to escape from something but rather to move closer toward Someone. The purpose of pilgrimage is not to run from God or others, but to be led by the Spirit into a richer relationship with both. The further you try to separate yourself from God, the closer you actually come to finding God, or God finding you, and in turn the closer you are to finding yourself. Sometimes to do so it is necessary to take leave of the world for a time and to sequester yourself in a sacred space of your own choosing, or God's leading. There you can listen in stillness and silence to the voice of God as the Spirit speaks, at times barely audibly, softly whispering the message of divine love into your soul.

We left the cell and returned to where we had begun, outside of the Abbey at St. Oran's Chapel. This mirrored the life of modern-day pilgrims who journeyed to Iona only for a short time and would return home to begin again. Just as our group separated and went our own ways, our hearts pondering this time together, so too those who took the trek to Iona would return to the places from whence they came, having been forever impacted by the journey.

I believe the pilgrimage isn't merely a walking tour of significant places and events on Iona, but also serves as a microcosm of a much greater life pilgrimage. Though we may live under the illusion of permanence and cling, sometimes desperately, to people, places, or empty hopes and dreams of the past, eventually, we all must leave and move on. Detaching from all that we hold dear in this world is not only part of the purpose of pilgrimage, but also an important preparation for our future. The more we have, the more difficult it is to do so. I had detached myself from my previous life and ventured into this new one. I did not know where I was going, but I knew God was leading me. To arrive at where I needed to be, I had to let go of all that I was holding onto and leave it behind. We are all on a journey to return to the origin of our being. It is non-negotiable, we all must leave life as we know it, and enter another place that awaits us, and most likely is beyond anything we can imagine.

As the pilgrimage concluded and the group dispersed, I trudged back up the hill to my room. As I did so this prayer by Thomas Merton came to mind.

> My Lord God, I have no idea where I am going. I do not see
> the road ahead of me. I cannot know for certain where it will
> end. Nor do I really know myself, and the fact that I think I am

following your will does not mean that I am actually doing so. But I believe that the desire to please you does in fact please you. And I hope I have that desire in all that I am doing. I hope that I will never do anything apart from that desire. And I know that if I do this you will lead me by the right road, though I may know nothing about it. Therefore, I will trust you always though I may seem to be lost and in the shadow of death. I will not fear, for you are ever with me, and you will never leave me to face my perils alone.[2]

It is the prayer of a pilgrim. It is the prayer that would give comfort to me and many others with whom I would share in the years to come.

---

2 Thomas Merton, *Thoughts in Solitude* (The Abbey of our Lady of Gethsemani, 1956) 79.

SIXTEEN

A Loving Farewell

As Columba laid down his books and the security of
the monastery,
> *So we lay down what is past and look to the future.*

As Brigid, with a cross of rushes, comforted a stranger,
> *So we take into daily life signs of hope and healing.*

As Patrick traveled ever on, as Margaret built community,
> *So we reach beyond ourselves, to share the lives of others
> and touch a wider world.*

> — "The Leaving Service" in *The Iona Abbey Worship Book*

Every week for nine weeks, I recited those words during the Friday morning Leaving Service. It was intended for guests, who would depart that day after spending a week on the island, and for volunteers, who would leave the following Wednesday after a lengthier stay. The Leaving Service applied to all, and soon, it would apply to me. I had often thought about what it was like for those guests and volunteers who, after spending a short season of their lives at Iona, were picking up their luggage and loading them onto the green van to be hauled back down to the jetty. What had they learned? What had they discovered about themselves? What spiritual souvenirs were they taking with them? And perhaps most significantly, what baggage were they leaving behind? The time was fast approaching to ask myself the same questions. What were the parts of my past that had washed up on the shore of Iona with me? What parts of me did I need to shed?

What meaningful aspects of this community could I now carry with me into a much wider world? Where would I ever find another surrogate family like this one? And perhaps most importantly, would this Divine Love accompany me, or would it also fade away and become a mere memory? As I waved farewell to the guests on that last Friday, the reality of my pending departure hit me like a strong gust of wind off the Sound. I could see my time approaching like a distant ship on the horizon, gradually making its way to the harbor. I had been one of those who had warmly welcomed others as they disembarked from the ferry and bid them farewell as they stepped back on; now, it would soon be my turn. It was time to prepare.

"Run, don't walk." That advice was given by my roommate Sam prior to his departure a few weeks earlier. I'd grown quite fond of him and missed him more than either of us could've imagined. It was good advice, not only for how to spend one's last days on the island, but also for how to navigate life.

Like a man who is being exiled from his own country, I squeezed as much as I could into every minute of every day before being forced to go home. I worked with more zeal and played with more zest. All my senses were on overdrive. I gave everything I had to give and, like a spiritual hoarder, took in everything I could take.

On that final Friday I made my way back from the jetty to the Abbey for the final center meeting. At the end of each of those meetings, staff members who were leaving were given the opportunity to share an insight from their time spent at Iona. When it was my turn, I shared an edited version of my story with those whom I shared my heart. I told of my divorce. I told of my struggles in the ministry. I told of leaving my previous life. I told of beginning a new one during my time at Iona. And finally, I told them how much I loved them all and how badly I would miss them. And as I told them, I wept. Abrahan was the first to hug me. Some spoke audibly, others only with their emotions. I hadn't experienced that degree of love from a community ever. Ever! The experience forever branded the inestimable value of living in a loving community. A feeling I would never forget. A truth I would never abandon.

I went on my way to perform the tasks awaiting me at the Abbey kitchen, moving like one of those ancient mourners must've as they traversed the Street of the Dead. Deeply immersed in my own melancholy, I moved mechanically moving through my morning routine, a welcome distraction to the dread which was filling me.

After work I took tea and scones with friends at the St. Columba Hotel. Our time ended much too soon. Returning to the lounge in my dorm, I reviewed my notes for the evening service. I had volunteered to speak, not because I missed the pulpit or preaching, but because I desired to stand in a space and experience something that heretofore had eluded me. Over the previous nine weeks a message had crystallized in my mind. It was so drastically different from anything I'd written before. There was no need to properly distinguish between certain doctrines, nor be dogmatic, nor point out the differences between "us" and "them." There was no pressure to impress parishioners with my knowledge and ability, nor to present information about God or the Bible that they never knew before. All that I wanted, and what I believed God wanted from me, was to speak a simple, genuine, heart-felt message to those whom I cared for deeply, whose hearts might be warmed, if not by the words that were spoken, at least by the love that conveyed them, based on my experience and observation of one of the activities most valued and practiced: knitting.

The message was based on the verse from Psalm 139 that says, "You were knit together in your mother's womb," and went something like this:

> "How good it is, how wonderful, to live together in community."
> That is true, most of the time. But sometimes there are challenges
> in daily living that aren't so wonderful, like sharing bathrooms
> and bedrooms with others, putting up with petty peeves of
> guests, trying to find space to have alone time or, when you do,
> having someone else invade that space. There are many challenges
> of living in community, but for me, one of the greatest has been
> knitting! In the process of trying to learn to knit, I've realized
> that knitting is a marvelous metaphor for life. We make a lot of

mistakes, and generally mess things up. Far too frequently we
don't know what we're doing, when we'll finish, or what we will
be when we do. But God does. God undoes all that we do wrong.
God is the master knitter. We are each God's wonderful knitting
project, a beautiful work in progress. How good it is to be knit
together in a community.

This message was therapeutic, for it was delivered to those whom I loved
and whom I knew had come to know and love me just for me. That was the
message that I had received from all of them throughout the entire time I
was at Iona.

Saturday began as usual with my personal devotion. It was based on
"The Journey of the Magi," the poem by T. S. Elliot in which one of the
travelers "retells the story." The last stanza reads as follows:

> All this was a long time ago, I remember,
> And I would do it again, but set down
> This set down
> This: were we led all that way for
> Birth or Death? There was a Birth, certainly.
> We had evidence and no doubt. I had seen birth
> And death,
> But had thought they were different. This Birth was
> Hard and bitter agony for us, like Death, our death.
> We returned to our places, these Kingdoms,
> But no longer at ease here, in the old dispensation,
> With an alien people clutching their gods.
> I should be glad of another death.

I remember studying that poem in my English literature class as a fresh-
man in college. It meant very little to me then. But now the significance
was staggering. The Magi had embarked on a life-changing journey, leaving
everything to find God. And in so doing, they found life and death, not
only His but theirs. In some way I felt that the poem described my journey.

I had found God not in a manger but in another unexpected place, a place where I found new life as well. And now, it was time to begin my journey home, a journey that represented both death and life.

My morning breakfast usually consisted of cornflakes, but on this Saturday, Deirdre prepared a "Scottish breakfast": eggs, beans, bacon, toast, black pudding, scones, and more. The resident staff hosted and served the volunteers. What a treat. It was the only time in ten weeks that I had enjoyed that luxury.

I had been asked by Simon, my supervisor, who had by now become like my adopted son, to do the reading for the evening service. It was taken from Genesis 18:1–8, which is the story of Abraham welcoming the three visitors. Again, God was speaking, reminding me and everyone there of the importance of hospitality. Iona was all about welcoming strangers, embracing them, as well as feeding and caring for them. Welcoming others is such a central idea that is repeated over and over in the Bible. Yet, it is one that is so frequently overlooked or ignored in the Christian church. To sincerely welcome and embrace others, regardless of what they look like, what they believe, how they act or dress or even smell—in other words, to welcome those as God has welcomed us is a gift of grace.

After the service, there was a gathering for game-playing in the MacLeod lounge. We let loose that night. Iona gave us the freedom to *be*; to *be* silly, silent, or serious, to *be* happy or heavy-hearted, to *be* old or young, to *be* who we believe we were meant to *be*, who God invited us to *be*.

Sunday marked my last Lord's Day at Iona. I spent most of the morning service simply gazing out the East Window. I was roused from the silent revelry by the sound of "Gabriel's Oboe," the theme song from the movie *The Mission*. It was being played as a musical interlude during the communion part of the service. The melody had been played on the cello at a few Good Friday services in my previous congregation. The movie and song meant so much more to me now, closely connected to Abrahan from Paraguay. It was a reminder of guided and gracious serendipity; assurance of the Divine Presence in this place.

Monday was my last day of work. But before I began, God spoke yet again during my morning meditation, this time through the words of the prophet Isaiah: "Do not recall the things of old or remember the things of the past." Iona had given me, as it did so many others, the opportunity to leave behind the broken remnants of my past which, with me, had washed up on shore. The challenge would be to not wade back into the cold, dark waters seeking to retrieve and relive all that had happened before. The Ceilidh that night was a final reminder to keep on celebrating, even when one didn't feel like it. For it was certain that God would send someone to take me by the hand and gently guide me in The Dance.

My last full day on the island was Tuesday, July 14, which would've been my thirty-first wedding anniversary. That date had been assigned to me, not chosen. It was a sign that the God I had become reacquainted with at Iona, cared enough to be recognized in coincidental details. Following is the entry I wrote in my journal:

> *Happy Un-Anniversary to me! It would've been thirty-one years today! Six years divorced. Unbelievable! Am I healed? No. To paraphrase my mother, "Divorce (like death) is something you never get over but learn to live with." But I no longer live with the guilt and the shame, I no longer have the gnawing feeling in the pit of my stomach, I no longer live with regrets. Iona is resurrection for me! And today, this LAST day on the island marks for me the time to break forth from the tomb! For me, this time at Iona is not ending, it's just beginning.*

That day began with an early morning walk up Dun I, the "Hill of Iona." I stood looking out from this high place and thought of the Transfiguration account in the Bible. Jesus took Peter, James, and John up a high mountain also. There He changed before them, and they saw His heavenly glory. Peter, experiencing the euphoria of the eternal, wanted to build shelters and remain. But Jesus insisted they follow Him off the mountain and into the valley to face their death as well as His. On that mount of Transfiguration, Jesus wasn't the only one who changed, the disciples changed as well. The trajectory of their lives had been altered forever. So had mine. Iona had been my taste of heaven. I didn't want to leave. Yet, I instinctively recognized that it was time to resume the journey and re-engage. The words of one of my favorite hymns for the Day of Transfiguration came to mind: "'Tis Good Lord, to be here, but we cannot remain, so since Thou bid us leave the mount come with us to the plain."[1]

During my final morning service, God was again present and speaking clearly, this time in the words of the hymn "Be Thou My Vision." The fourth verse jumped off the page.

> Riches I heed not, nor man's empty praise,
> Thou mine inheritance, now and always;
> Thou and Thou only, first in my heart,
> High King of Heaven, my Treasure Thou art.

Here at Iona, I had re-discovered my true treasure. It had been hidden not on the island, but inside of me. All that I had left behind and sold, the price that was paid to make this happen, was all worth it. For me, it was the Pearl of Great Price. The hidden treasure of Divine Love, grace, and forgiveness that God places inside each of us is there, waiting for us to discover it as well. I would be taking those treasures with me as I left Iona. Nonetheless, after the service, I went off to purchase a few worldly treasures, some to give as parting gifts to those who were dear to me, like wool for my favorite knitters, a cross for Abrahan, and a few keepsakes for my family.

It was the tradition that those who were leaving would host a little farewell gathering. So, after dinner, we gathered in the Cul Shuna lounge for the party. There was no lack of laughter or tears. It was time to leave for the last evening service, the one devoted to healing.

Part of that service includes a special blessing and prayer for those volunteers or staff who are leaving. Elina, a volunteer who was also leaving, and I both wept not only during the prayers but throughout much of the service.

As a pastor I had shut down my emotions, trying to protect myself from my own feelings. I did everything I possibly could to avoid them. One of the seven deadly sins in the medieval church was Acedia. It comes from the

---

1 "'Tis Good Lord to Be Here," text by Joseph A. Robinson; tune by Johann Sebastian Bach.

Greek "a-kedos" which means "without care." To not feel, to not desire, to not want for anything is to deny one's basic humanity. Grief had caused me to drift into Acedia without knowing it. During the last years of my pastoral life, I had become numb. Numb not only to my pain but also the pain of others. I had become adept at putting on the cloak of compassion, which served as insulation against feeling. Despite being surrounded by suffering in various forms, I seldom if ever cried for others because it simply hurt too much to allow myself to feel the messiness of those emotions. I learned a kind of spiritual and emotional stoicism, a guardedness when it came to grief. I couldn't allow myself to empathetically join with others for fear of having my own feelings surface.

Iona changed that. It gave me permission to fully feel myriad emotions and provided a safe space to do so. There was no need to try and impress others, nor to protect myself from those who would interpret sadness as a sign of weakness. In only ten short weeks I had fallen in love with both the place and people. And now as I prepared to experience yet another separation, I allowed myself to fully grieve.

In the end, everyone was invited to come forward into the healing circle for the laying on of hands. I knelt before Simon, felt his hand on my shoulder, and heard him speak the words which I'd heard many times before, but now became deeply personal. "The Spirit of the Living God be upon you, and may you be healed of all that harms you in body, soul, and spirit. In the Name of Jesus. Amen." As Simon prayed those words over me, I could feel the Spirit of God come over me, filling me physically, emotionally, and spiritually. I was renewed. I hadn't been healed instantaneously, but gradually. My healing did not happen through a single laying on of hands in one service, but through the many loving hands that had been laid upon me during the time spent there.

At the service's conclusion, one last activity was planned, a fire on the North End beach. Many made the mile-and-a-half long walk that night. We sat around the fire and ate, drank, sang, and reminisced. Slowly people began to drift away, and the fire died out. At 1:30 a.m. the few of us who remained doused the last of the embers and slowly sauntered back to our small rooms on this small island which had become home. If home is where the heart is, then Iona was home to me.

Morning came too soon. I hurriedly shoved the few items I would be taking with me into my backpack, donned my Scotland Rugby shirt, took a few last photos of my living space, and descended the stairs, exiting the main doors of the MacLeod Center to hike down the hill one last time. My farewell walk took me to the small, nearly hidden back door of the Abbey, which led into a narrow dungeon-like corridor and up a narrow stone staircase. At the top of the stairs, I peered one last time into the large Abbey kitchen, before taking my final walk through it. I went into the scullery and large dining hall, my senses stimulated by the memories being replayed in my mind's eye. From there, I passed through the cloisters and into the church for one last look at the East Window. Exiting up the well-trodden steps, past the baptismal font, and through the large main doors, looming before me was the sight that first greeted me: St. Martin's Cross. As I passed by, I placed the last of my burdens at the foot of it. Back down the single-lane road I went walking toward the village. And then I paused again, this time in front of the cottage with the green door. But now it looked different. Now, it felt different. It had lost its power to plunge me into painful memories from my past. Now, it was a portal through which I would fearlessly step into the new, vibrant life that awaited me. I gave one final kiss to my old life, another to my new love, Iona, and a third to the Lover I had met there.

As I arrived at the jetty, others were already gathered, most of whom had become my family. God was there in the midst of them, smiling in the warm sunshine reflected in the water and dancing on the waves. I knew that I would never again see most of these people this side of eternity, and so I gifted them with the words that I had heard from them and seen in them; the only words that mean anything, and in the end, the words that mean everything. "I love you."

We were still saying our farewells when the ferry arrived. Tearing myself away, I bought my ticket and boarded the boat. Ascending to the upper deck, I got a better view of those who were staying. We waved. And we waved. And we waved some more. And as I stood on the ferry deck, watching them recede in my sight, I wept yet again. I watched as they faded into the distance, slowly walking away to resume the familiar routine that had become such an important part of my life for such a short time. I already missed them. They were resuming their daily lives, and I was embarking on a new one. As the ferry moved farther from shore, I realized how small this island that had been my world for the past ten weeks really was. Yet it had made such a magnificent difference in my life.

If there is an experience of being "born again," mine occurred on that tiny little outcropping of rock. I felt as if I was mostly dead inside before arriving at Iona. The ten weeks on the island completed the process. Sometime during my stay, I had completely died—at least the person that had stepped foot there had. The grief, guilt, shame, and overwhelming sense of failure that I had brought with me had been washed away, replaced with the grace, mercy, and forgiveness of a Loving God. Regret had been replaced with gratitude not only for my time in Iona, but for everything and everyone that had taken me there. Surely, this is what resurrection felt like. As I watched Iona recede into the distance, I thought I caught a glimpse of that old part of me making his way along the beach. I could barely recognize him, as he had become a stranger. I could hardly see him, his shadowy silhouette vaguely visible. He seemed to be wading into the surf. And then he quickly faded from view and vanished. Gone forever.

Part Four

EPILOGUE

Loving Iona

WHEREVER YOU ARE GOING, BE IT NEAR OR FAR,
UNTIL YOU RETURN TO IONA, BE IONA WHEREVER YOU ARE.
—Michael, an Iona volunteer

Friday, the thirteenth day of May 2022. Not unlucky at all. In fact, just the opposite, My fourth trip to Iona. It's been seven years (the number of completion) since I left the last time. Even though my spiritual pilgrimage continues, I feel content, complete, centered. Iona placed me on this path, which, like the Celtic view of time and space, is circular. I continue to orbit around this holy place, this time returning not as a curious tourist or as a broken pastor in need of healing but as a beloved child who has missed his Beloved. It's so good to be back in the warm embrace of the place I love, in the arms of the One who loves me.

Familiar sites have met me on the return trip. I ride the same train from Glasgow to Oban, the same bus to Fionnphort, the same ferry carries me across the sound to Iona, the brilliant blue waters waving a warm welcome to me. I walk through the same sleepy island village and past the same ruins of the Nunnery, up the same narrow road that leads to St. Oran's Chapel and the cemetery, past St. Columba's Hill and St. Martin's Cross, and finally through the doors of the same old Abbey. It is all so familiar, so comforting. It feels like coming home.

And yet, there is something unfamiliar about the place. For all that is so similar, so much has changed. The living quarters in the Abbey have been renovated. The old stone floors are covered with new laminate hardwood that leads to a refurbished refectory and remodeled guest rooms. There is an elevator that makes the upper floor accessible for those who are disabled. The common room has a new fireplace and furniture, replacing the old charm with more modern comfort. It is pleasant in a sterile kind of way. The scullery has an automatic dishwasher and sanitizer, an entirely new way of washing the dishes. Outside, the old village hall has been demolished, and a new one with much more room has been built to take its place. The MacLeod Center, where I stayed, is closed. Most striking of all, perhaps, is the absence of the house with the green door.

Not only has the place changed, but so have the people. The volunteer housekeepers, cooks, and those leading the services are all strangers. Where are the familiar faces that made the place so welcoming? Where are Abrahan, Britt, Simon, and my other old friends? This place is not the same without them. I feel like the grown-up child who returns home only to discover that their parents have sold the house to someone else who has moved in and remodeled it.

But why am I surprised? For I have changed also. I am not the same person who washed up on these shores seven years ago. I spent only a short time at this sacred place, but Iona transformed me. I carry with me more than memories, the rich spiritual tapestry which the holy isle wove within me will remain forever. I have been gifted with a new perspective on life itself that began to gain clarity the moment I followed the call to forsake all and step forth into the world that is Iona.

Rather than merely knowing *about* God, I now *know* God, at least as best I can. Better yet, I am known by God. Prior to going to Iona, I knew a lot about God, or at least thought I did. I spent twenty-seven years doing my absolute best to theologically define and dogmatize God. The more I learned about God, the greater my ego grew and the smaller my God became. It was a process in which God was put into a box, wrapped neatly and nicely, and delivered to those sitting in a big container called "church." Iona changed that. Iona allowed me to move in and with this beautiful mystery of God. Iona reintroduced me to my Loving God. Iona freed me to live in, with, and under God's gracious love.

At Iona I experienced the love of God not as a theological concept that I preached about, but as the gift of grace that was given me. Grace is God's love in action in the form of mercy, kindness, forgiveness, generosity, and hospitality that is put into practice by everyday people. Grace is the Loving God with skin on. Grace is the humility found in humans to love and accept others, not as we want them to be, or think they should be, but as they are, and to do the same for ourselves. Like us, grace is a precious diamond in the rough. Grace is believing that God really does love us just as we are and doesn't demand or command that we try to be something or someone else. What matters is the love of the Giver, not the actions, attitude, or the aptitude of the receiver. Loving grace comes disguised in the dirt, the grime, and the grit of our lives and the lives of other people just like us. And it is quite likely that the very elements of our lives that we consider most shameful and feel most guilty about serve as the receptacles into which gracious love is poured, and from which we pour the same out upon others. God's Love is a gift, not a divine transaction. There is no quid pro quo associated with gracious love. It is given without manipulation and void of any expectation. We don't have to do something more, give something extra, or become someone else, to illustrate our worthiness in getting, or gratitude in receiving such a great gift. Loving grace is a heavenly cornucopia from which all the compassion, care, and kindness of God that can possibly be contained overflows, and from which we are lovingly allowed to consume as much as we possibly can. Grace is the fountain of loving forgiveness from which we are tenderly invited to drink to our heart's content. Loving grace overflows into the cracked pots that appear as our lives so that we can in turn try to fill the leaking cisterns of others. There's an endless amount of God's love, so we don't need to hoard it or be stingy in its distribution. God's love comes at us from every direction and from no direction at all. It is the gift of God gained and garnered by the Christ and given abundantly through the Spirit.

Here's the thing about God's loving grace; at the end of the day, it can't be adequately described or defined. I spent years of my pastoral life trying to do so. But all the theology in the world couldn't save me when I desperately needed grace. Grace, like God, must be experienced. And the best time to experience loving grace is when we mistakenly believe that we are in a godless and graceless place in our lives. It is then that God makes an unexpected appearance, perhaps disguised as an enormous problem or a desperately dark place, and then ambushes us in the form of a kind and compassionate Spirit who takes us gently by the hand and accompanies us on a path God very well might use to recreate us and remake our lives, to lovingly give us a life that is almost beyond our imagination. Kind of like the God giving it. I experienced Divine loving grace in its fullness at Iona, and I believe it was the most valuable gift I received.

Granted, there was so much more that I took with me from Iona, some of which I've written about here, some of which I'm aware and reminded of on a regular basis, and some of which I am completely unaware, as it is so deeply enmeshed within that it has simply become part of me. Some of this must remain a mystery, and a very personal one at that. And so, I will refrain from writing more, hoping that you either have or will experience the transformational love of God, which, whether it occurs at Iona or elsewhere, will lead you on a journey to discover your own Belovedness.

On my last day on the island, I decided to make the familiar pilgrimage to St. Columba's Bay. The weather was cold and rainy. The path was a familiar one. At the beach, I climbed the same outcropping of rocks that I had sat on before. And yet, it felt very different. I decided to re-enact the ritual that had meant so much to me before. I picked up a rock, symbolizing the burdens that I was carrying. This one was much smaller than the one I had previously chosen all those years before. It was the size of my little fingernail. I tossed it softly into the water. And then I picked up a few more, not for myself, but for others. I didn't need to carry a rock to remind me of Iona, for I was carrying Iona deep inside of myself. The ritual now signified the new person I had become. The Spirit of the Wild Goose, of the Living and Loving God, was inside me. Iona had worked its magic on me, like it had so many others. It had called me to return to the island, to God, and to myself. Though I was leaving, I could be sure that I would return again and again to this sacred place. And I was just as certain that I would take it with me.

I stayed there for a time to breathe in both my previous experience and the one I was currently having. And then I began the walk back to the Abbey for the evening service, through the green fields, past the sheep and the cattle. It was the end of a brilliant day of sunshine, the radiant rays of which were making their final farewell to the day. As I rounded a small bend in the road, the Abbey came into full view, and though it wasn't raining, I was met with the sight of a beautiful rainbow perfectly framing her. During all the time I spent at Iona, I'd never seen such a sight. Here was one last love note, a Divine sign of God's promise of restoration and resurrection. It was the promise of a new life that had, on the one hand, already commenced and on the other was only just beginning.

Acknowledgments

This book began as jottings in a journal. Over a period of eight years, it expanded and took on many iterations, from a therapeutic effort to deal with the grief of leaving Iona, to a personal memoir that finally exorcised the pain of my past, to an attempt to be an inspirational work intended to give hope to all those, clergy and others, who are or have been in the dark places I traveled. I never intended to go public with it, but thanks to a few dear friends whom I trusted to read the rough draft, I was led to do so. I am especially grateful to Gregg Gonzales who gave me the final nudge and connected me with Susie Schaefer, who made the mystery of publishing come to life. I am also grateful to Erik Evenson, who did an initial edit, and assured me that it had value to someone other than myself, and Bethany Good, who did the final edit and was invaluable in making corrections and suggestions so that it wouldn't read like a sermon.

Of course, I'm grateful to all those in the Iona Community, especially those I lived and loved with during my short time there. Some have been mentioned by name, with their permission, others have had their names changed, and many others remain unnamed. All of them served as beacons of light, illuminating my heart with the love of God.

I am grateful to all those over the years who put up with me as their pastor. I'm sorry and ask your forgiveness for any spiritual harm I caused. Be assured it was unintentional. Thanks to all of those who helped shape me during my many years of ministry. You were doing God's work. I'm grateful to those who made my life as a pastor difficult, who helped lead me to the ledge and encouraged me to jump. You made it possible for me to experience death and resurrection. And thanks to all of those friends and colleagues who faithfully stood with me during those dark and desolate times, Chris, Margaret, Ernestine, Andrew, Larry, Vera, Claude, Donna, Cliff, Lu, Greg, Rob, and many others. You know who you are.

And of course, thanks to my family. To Mom and Dad, who I am convinced continue to guide me. To my surrogate father Ernie, and my father in The Faith, Lester. To my daughters, who I dragged all over the world and subjected to way too many hours spent in church and without their father. You are my heart. I thank you for your love, and forgiveness. And to the saints of Allenspark Community Church, who restored my faith in "church."

References

Keating, Thomas. *Invitation to Love: The Way of Christian Contemplation*. London: Bloomsbury Publishing, 2011.

MacLeod, Fiona. *Celtic Daily Prayer: Prayers and Readings from the Northumbria Community*. HarperOne, 2002.

McIntosh, Kenneth. *Water from an Ancient Well: Celtic Spirituality for Modern Life*. Vestal, NY: Anamchara Books, 2011.

Merton, Thomas. *Thoughts in Solitude*. Abbey of Our Lady of Gethsemani, 1956.

Newell, J. Philip. *Listening for the Heartbeat of God: A Celtic Spirituality*. London: SPCK Publishing, 2008.

Nouwen, Henri. *The Inner Voice of Love: A Journey Through Anguish to Freedom*. Doubleday, 1996.

O'Donohue, John. *Walking in Wonder: Eternal Wisdom for a Modern World*. New York: Convergent Books, 2015.

Rohr, Richard. *Falling Upward: A Spirituality for the Two Halves of Life*. Hoboken, NJ: Jossey-Bass, 2011.

The Iona Community. *Iona Abbey Worship Book*. Glasgow: Wild Goose Publications, 2002.

Weller, Francis. *The Wild Edge of Sorrow: Ritual and Renewal and the Sacred Work of Grief*. Berkeley, CA: North Atlantic Books, 2015

About the Author

The son of Jean and Ralph Patrick, both of whom have completed their life journey, Ralph was raised in northern Wisconsin, which birthed in him his love of God as experienced in nature. Ralph is a father to four wonderful daughters with whom he loves spending quality time. Ralph's passions include hiking, reading, writing, and traveling, especially to Scotland and Cambodia.

Ralph has served in various roles, including inner city pastor, overseas missionary, and as a director for two non-profit organizations. He has volunteered for numerous philanthropic agencies, including the Iona Community and the Ray of Hope ministry for children in Cambodia. Some of the proceeds of this book will go to each of those. Most recently, Ralph worked as a Regional Director in the Colorado chapter of the Alzheimer's Association and serves a small faith community in Colorado. His passion is helping others as a spiritual director, motivational speaker, and dementia consultant through Cardinal Crossroads, an organization he started to honor his mother.

He has a B.A. from Concordia University, St. Paul; a M.Div. from Concordia Theological Seminary, Fort Wayne; and a M.Th. from Glasgow University, Scotland.

To learn more about Ralph, visit TheCelticCompass.com